HARMONIOUS HOME

HARMONIOUS HOME

SMART PLANNING FOR A HOME THAT REALLY WORKS

JUDITH WILSON

photography by Jan Baldwin

RYLAND
PETERS
& SMALL

LONDON NEW YORK

First published in the United Kingdom
in 2004 by Ryland Peters & Small
Kirkman House
12–14 Whitfield Street
London W1T 2RP
www.rylandpeters.com

10 9 8 7 6 5 4 3 2 1

Text © Judith Wilson 2004
Design and photographs
© Ryland Peters & Small 2004

ISBN 1 84172 599 4

A CIP record for this book is available
from the British Library.

Printed and bound in China

Senior editor Clare Double
Location research Claire Hector,
Judith Wilson
Production Patricia Harrington

Art director Gabriella Le Grazie
Publishing director Alison Starling

Styling Judith Wilson

contents

opposite **Take a mental virtual-reality tour of your ideal home, and think through every possible day-to-day (and evening) activity for each member of the household. Ask yourself what your living space doesn't cater for, which a newly planned one might? Aesthetically, the space shown here is modern and slick, yet also boasts well-planned sociable zones to suit an active family.**

introduction

We all long for a harmonious home. That is, a tempting space where colour and texture blend seamlessly and each room has a visual connection with the next. A home so well planned you can chat on the phone while stirring supper, where task lights are aptly placed, and there's always a connection for the laptop. Even better, one whose space configuration perfectly matches your lifestyle, be that flexible areas for socializing, or a tiny cottage for two. In today's busy world, tailor-made space isn't a luxury. It's a necessity.

Yet, just as every lifestyle is unique, there's only one individual (give or take accompanying professionals) who can guarantee a personalized environment – and that is you. So take responsibility for it. It's tempting to blame your home's previous owners for ill-placed radiators, or no sunlight on the stairs. In an ideal world, we'd all reach design nirvana with a new-build home. The reality is to tweak the 'bare bones' of the property already at your disposal. Make it the goal to personalize your home. Plan for that now, and you're en route to a bespoke environment.

How much it costs is down to personal budget, timescale and your vision of a harmonious home. What's important is to think through why an existing home isn't working, and how it may be altered. Is the lighting system antiquated? Do tiny rooms cramp the family's style? Must you run from room to room to answer the phone? Time and money spent addressing these fundamental issues will reap benefits later. So resolve to get the shell right first, rather than opting for the quick cosmetic fix of fresh paint or new curtains. Decoration will never disguise the annoyance of insufficient plug sockets, or lack of music in the bathroom.

Apply these early thought processes across the whole home, not just to random rooms. Typically, we focus attention on a kitchen that needs revamping, or invest in a new bathroom. But reviewing the entire home saves time and money in the long run: it's simpler to plan and budget for upgrades or building work en masse, rather than jobs done piecemeal. So begin by looking at your home's services, its architectural good and bad points, the exterior and its layout. Think of it as a home health-check.

And when it's time for decorative decisions, the whole-home approach makes light work of creating a cohesive scheme. Many of us plan individual rooms, with little thought to how everything hangs together visually. Yet the dynamic of any home is that we travel constantly through it, catching glimpses from room to room, even moving furniture between spaces. So it makes sense to pick a limited palette of colours and surfaces, which can be reinterpreted around the house, giving balance and contrast.

Harmonious Home will help you plan. In Thoughts and Plans, there are prompts for evaluating the lifestyle you have and whether that matches your home, and hints on crystallizing your decorative vision. Bare Essentials is an overview of the crucial services you need, from lighting to plumbing, and points the way to picking a decorating palette that pleases the eye. And in Space Specifics, there are space options to help you decide what sort of rooms you need, and why. Time spent planning a tailor-made home shouldn't be a chore, but a pleasure. Enjoy the ride.

this page **Even if not all are executed at once, considering plans for your whole home, rather than room by room, creates more flexible options. In this ground-floor apartment, plenty of storage has been fitted seamlessly around the stairwell and above the adjacent door, cleverly compensating for lack of cupboards in an existing small bedroom.**

thoughts and plans

A strong concept is the springboard for potential change. It's also an essential reference point as plans progress from inspirations to practicalities. So gather as many ideas as possible, remembering that gut reactions and early thoughts are often best. These will form the groundwork for your harmonious home.

examining the raw potential

In the beginning, it's vital to take a long, cool look at your property, warts and all. If you are moving, make this part of the buying process. If reassessing an existing home, then try to look at it with fresh eyes. The gathering of swatches and furniture catalogues – the decorating part – comes later. What matters first is to concentrate on what you have now. Only when you've investigated the building's potential can you make decisions about which features to retain or alter, and to what extent the original fabric of the building will inspire a decorative scheme.

First look at what architects call the 'bare bones' of the building. What are its architectural strong points? Consider not just the larger features, from windows to flooring, but finer details like cornices, skirting boards or ceiling beams. How much of it is original, or is there a patchwork of styles? If something is in bad condition, will you restore or replace? Apply these questions just as much to a Seventies apartment as to a listed Georgian house. What matters is not period authenticity, but whether features work with the space you have.

Think, too, about whether the existing division of rooms suits you. Will room functions need to be shifted, or walls knocked down? This is particularly relevant if you are buying a new property. Getting the 'envelope' right in the first place is not only a time saver, but makes financial sense too.

this picture **A dominant architectural feature, such as a beamed attic roof, will often dictate space planning. Here, the 'spare' space beneath the pitch was the ideal spot to locate a chair and desk for quiet study.**

left Use the 'bones' of the space to inspire a decorative scheme, rather than trying to impose a different style on it. Open-tread staircases and exposed rafters in a loft, say, suggest an informal, zoned living area.

below In a period property, you have choices. Either pick authentic furnishings to match the architectural detailing, or – a more modern option – keep upholstery and furniture simple, to cast attention on great windows or an aged floor.

left **Thinking laterally around problematical features, such as fixed ceiling beams, can provoke dramatic solutions. In this property, conventional low-voltage downlighters weren't possible, but chic angled spotlights are.**

below left **Unusual proportions may also prompt a decorative theme. The tranquil mood in this bedroom derives from a few simple, scaled-up pieces of furniture, picked to echo the tall ceiling.**

below right **A striking pair of doors, or an unusual window, can provide decorative inspiration for themed joinery throughout the home.**

A well-planned property should feel comfortably balanced. So walk around it and consciously observe whether the space feels right. Windows and doors must appear in proportion to the room size, ceiling heights be consistent, and rooms flow easily off the main traffic areas. You'll notice if a staircase bisects a small cottage uncomfortably, or if a room has been divided up unsympathetically. If there is much to remedy, ask an architect for a one-off consultation. He/she will advise on how to readjust a property to its original proportions, or adapt an old building to fit a modern lifestyle.

Look, too, at the exterior of the property. If the inside lacks a distinctive architectural character, perhaps there is unusual brickwork or shingling outside that might be repeated as a decorative theme within. Consider whether there's free-flowing access from indoors to outside. Might new French doors or a relocated back door be a good idea? Also think about the junction of materials between outside and in. Are there links, such as an original tiled floor from kitchen to terrace, which might be played up or extended?

If structural work is the answer to making the space work for you, then find a great architect or builder, call in quotes, and make those changes. They might include installing plumbing in a spare room (to convert it into an en suite bathroom), knocking down a wall (to create an open-plan kitchen/diner) or embarking on a loft extension (to create more bedrooms). Isn't it better to invest in the shell now, and save for the decorative touches?

this page **Is the exterior of the property more interesting architecturally than the features within? Then consider making key materials, from rough brick to tongue-and-groove panelling, part of the interior scheme as well, to provide character where none existed before. The continuity of materials makes for a seamless visual connection between outside and in, especially if a single colour scheme is repeated throughout.**

Think about the junction of materials between outside and in. Are there links which might be played up or extended?

lifestyle and human traffic flow

this page **Fuss-free living includes addressing things that are intrinsic to your lifestyle. Think of the home computer, the bikes, the kids' school kit, and more. Plan for them, and they become part of the grand living scheme; ignore their presence, and they get in the way.**

opposite **In an open-plan space, furniture layout makes the difference between good and bad traffic flow. Position heavy, permanent pieces to one side of commonly used areas. Then add chairs or screens, which can be used to section off cosier zones when relaxing or entertaining.**

It's easy to focus on achieving a great-looking interior, forgetting that the best living space must also function like a dream for its occupants. Rooms are rarely static spaces. On a daily basis, we shift in and out, make a mess, tidy up, invite in visitors, and expect to relax. Activity is the lifeblood of a home, so planning for it should be priority number one, not an afterthought. Without a thorough understanding of how you and your family want to live, no home can be truly tailor-made. For designers and architects, lifestyle is always the starting point. So make it yours too.

Begin by investing in a binder with dividers, so notes can be amassed as your plans and observations progress. If there's a big family, quiz each member about what constitutes their ideal home. If you share with a partner, what does he/she long for? Their opinions matter as much as yours do. Obvious though it sounds, it's vital to note down how many live at home, including 'floating' inhabitants: kids at college who return during holidays, stepchildren at weekends, or regular guests. The latter affects the number of bedrooms, as well as the size of congregation areas.

Focus, too, on when home is at its busiest. Do you work from home? Is this a family house with small children and visitors coming in and out all day? Or is it an evenings- and weekends-only retreat for a career-minded couple? The answers will directly affect whether the key living areas maximize on daylight and an open-plan layout, or if the emphasis is on ambient, seating areas for entertaining and relaxing by night. Make a separate list of how you like to socialize. Intimate dinner parties call for a great dining area, whereas eating out every night may dictate a small, no-frills kitchen for preparing the occasional TV dinner.

A detailed lifestyle analysis doesn't just crystallize the ideal room configuration at home. Your answers can be referred back to when planning storage (how many CDs, do you love clothes?), lighting (tranquil, or task lights?), or home technology (how many will use a computer, and where?). It will also help with decorative choices, such as whether new surfaces must be hard-wearing, if yours is a busy household, or if high-maintenance, but beautiful, fabrics and wall-coverings are an option.

Now consider the practicalities of human traffic flow around the house. Start off by sketching floor plans (they don't need to be to scale). Rough out the layout of rooms on each level, and show linking areas, including entrances and exits, the hall, staircase and landings. Use arrows to show which areas are busiest, and at what times: bedrooms to a shared bathroom, for example, or the kitchen to front door. If busy areas are problematical (a narrow corridor, say, or lack of access to outdoors), this may cue plans for building work. Less radically, extra storage may provide an answer, perhaps streamlining a small hall.

Repeat the sketches and arrows for individual rooms. Within each, there will be well-trodden routes, from door to sofa, or from cooker to dining table. Only when you understand these can you dream up the most user-friendly furniture layout. Think through specific activities, too. If people are watching TV, is there somewhere to put a drink? Is there a place to sit close by the phone? Can you

opposite **If a staircase bisects an open-plan area, prevent it dominating the space by picking one with open or glass treads, or team with a glass landing.**

above **Pay attention to the visual impact of halls and corridors. Furnished with slim pieces, and well lit (with at least some natural light), they give the illusion of practical, streamlined rooms.**

read in the bath, and is there a place for your book? The answer to these specific queries will help to fine-tune the process of planning where lighting, telephone and heating must go.

Spare a thought for the needs of guests or frequent visitors. It can be helpful here to mentally divide home into private areas (the home office, family bedrooms, en suite bathrooms) and public spaces (entertaining rooms, the cloakroom, a

guest bedroom). It's much nicer if visitors needn't traipse past the kids' playroom in order to use the loo, or if the au pair can have friends round without them clattering past your own bedroom door. Investing in a new ground-floor toilet, however tiny, or locating one spare bedroom below the level of the family's bedrooms, can make all the difference to seamless living.

Lastly, remember that movement around the house inevitably creates noise. Think of children clattering on the stairs, people talking on portable phones, and so on. Today's obsession with open-plan living areas, not to mention double-height halls or mezzanine floors, makes noise control (and privacy) even more of an issue. So take steps to reduce sound levels. Stairs may be enclosed, perhaps with an additional door between floors. Panelled doors linking hall and living area, a 'window' section in walls between rooms, or sliding doors pressed into service only when peace is needed are also tricks to employ.

LIFESTYLE CHECKLIST

- Define your 'home' personality. Does your lifestyle demand a tidy, busy, tranquil or cosy space?
- How many live here? Do numbers swell at weekends/holidays?
- How sociable are you? Is there room for parties?
- Where does everyone naturally congregate?
- Do you need quiet rooms, as well as activity spaces?
- Is this a daytime home, or an evening retreat?
- Are you usually at home on weekends, or away? An indoors or outdoors fan?

Spare a thought for the needs of visitors. It can be helpful here to mentally divide home into private areas and public spaces.

above **The square hall, with key rooms opening directly off it, remains one of the most sociable arrangements in an active home.**

opposite **The layout of many mansion flats, with their elegant** *enfilades* **of rooms, is also ideal for improving traffic flow.**

budget, resources and timing

No project, however small, can progress without an honest and detailed evaluation of budget. Even if you begin with ballpark estimates, start by comparing the potential cost of what you'd like to achieve, versus the money on tap right now. Don't guess – get the calculator out and do the sums. There's nothing like seeing figures written out to concentrate the mind. Remember, whether you're ordering a few made-to-measure blinds, or rewiring the entire house, costs frequently soar above initial estimates, so plan for that. Any working budget needs constant review.

right **Designers concur that the majority of a budget should go on getting the shell of a building right first; that is, the ideal space configuration, pretty architectural features, efficient services. If finances are tight later on, then make savings by choosing lower-spec materials or cheaper fabrics.**

If initial calculations seem achievable, then amass detailed quotes. Shop around for two or three estimates, because prices vary enormously. Also listen out for recommendations. A more expensive builder or electrician may deliver on time, and a cheaper outfit might drag the work on. It's always better to spend money on quality workmanship, using inexpensive materials, than vice versa, because the finished article will look more polished.

If moving house is the target, there's more to budget for. There are inevitable fees, surveys and so on. Think about 'hidden' costs, from removal services to reconnecting the phone. If structural work is necessary, decide now if you can invest in an architect, or use a good builder working to your own designs. Though expensive, an architect can save money by maximizing the use of the space, and time, by negotiating with planning departments. Contact the RIBA for advice on hiring one.

Think laterally if figures for the ultimate vision are way off the money available. First, investigate

methods to bump up the finance. Will remortgaging free a lump sum? What about a home improvement loan? And balance the amount spent on a property versus the area it's in. However wonderful it is, the cost of, say, underfloor heating in a run-down city area won't recoup its value once you move on.

Don't be disheartened if plans appear too grand for the available money. There are ways to retain the spirit of a scheme, while slashing budgets. A designer kitchen can be copied by a joiner, or a fabulously planned lighting system realized with DIY centre fittings. Doing the research and sourcing may take longer, but makes for a more creative brief. This is a good time to assess design priorities. If a slate floor throughout will, in your opinion, be the major link for creating a harmonious home, then invest a generous portion in it, and scale down quality of fittings elsewhere.

Think back to the raw potential at home. What resources here will reduce costs? For example, resanding and waxing existing boards will cost

left **Careful budgeting help to prioritize choices. For example, an elegant finish may be achieved by investing in solid wood joinery throughout, while savings are made on inexpensive neutral carpeting.**

right **The more seamless your final design vision, the more investment is necessary to conceal services. Here, discreet underfloor heating grilles and an integrated fridge provide a truly minimal modern kitchen.**

much less than a new floor. Adding fashionable doors to existing cupboards, in the same style throughout, will unify the property.

No budget overview is complete without considering timescale. Too tight a schedule, and money is wasted paying workmen overtime, or redoing rushed work. Too long, and your life will be disrupted; if you're staying in a rental property, it will cost a fortune. Considering timing and budget concurrently helps prioritize. If there isn't the finance to complete every stage now, what work is most important? How long can you wait for the rest?

BUDGET, RESOURCES AND TIMING CHECKLIST

- What's your budget? Can it be extended? If so, how and by how much?
- If moving house, list costs from estate agents' fees to hidden extras.
- If doing building work, can you afford an architect or builder? Commissioning an architect for plans only is cheaper.
- How much time do you have? Do you need a project manager?
- What's your ideal schedule? Is it feasible to work in stages?
- Set aside at least 10% of your budget for furnishing.
- List all existing features that can be adapted or restored to save funds.

right **Expensive materials, such as marble or solid wood, need only be used sparingly throughout a home to create an overall impression of luxury.**

As planning progresses and with budget and lifestyle facts to hand, it becomes more realistic to firm up those final goals of decorative finishes, visual impact and ambience at home. It's easier to assess whether cream silk curtains will be a recurrent theme, or if practical plywood and concrete surfaces are the order of the day. What mood do you want: welcoming, casual, or chic? Is the aim for pared-down, sleek surfaces or a bohemian mix? Only when these thoughts are clear can you start to construct a homogeneous look throughout the space.

goals and expectations

So return to the original visual concept and flesh it out. Keep things general, thinking in categories that include ambience, colour flow, balance of light and dark, and decorative themes (pared-down, dressed-up, funky), rather than tying yourself down to specific room schemes. Then look through interiors magazines with these concepts in mind, noting which rooms attract you (and why) and amassing tear sheets. A picture that captures a distinctive mood can be as useful for crystallizing goals as details of where to source taps. The more looking and musing takes place, the stronger your approach when choosing specific colours and surfaces.

Focusing on the ultimate goal now makes sense because it affects decisions about lighting, heating and more. If you're after statement decorating, then state-of-the-art lighting and trendy finishes need to

It's a planning conundrum that you must devise a visual concept long before amassing colours and accessories. Think of it as layering. *opposite* **A pretty cornice is a building block for a sophisticated drawing room; while** *above* **a glass shower door and skylight enhance a stairwell's contours.**

be found and installed. A low-key, simple finish, with maximum natural light and original bathroom fittings, requires fewer alterations, but needs well-planned decoration to play up the wholesome mood.

So define your own interpretation of the bespoke home. For some, it will indeed mean a choice of light switches, so bedroom lamps can be turned off

left **The chance to add an extension guarantees a tailor-made space. This one uses stepped floor levels, and a built-in bench and desk, to satisfy many different activity needs.**

below **Don't overlook the importance of detailing in the final stages, to realize decorative goals. The green foliage outside the dining-room windows has been linked to this colour scheme with emerald silk curtain lining.**

opposite **Aim for essential contrast at the core of every home: dark and light, big and small, smooth and rough. Here, it is the tonal shifts between walls and floors that create the visual juxtaposition.**

from in bed or by the door. But others, who enjoy the quirkiness of an old property, will positively enjoy the natural rhythm of an antiquated boiler that takes time to heat bath water, and focus instead on a cohesive visual flow. For those who like to reinvent their living space on a regular basis, emphasis will be on open-plan spaces that can adapt to new furniture configurations.

And whether the aim is for a no-frills bachelor pad, or a luxurious grown-up home, adopt a perfectionist's mindset now. It's always hard to maintain attention to detail throughout. But there's no point planning stunning inset lights in a cherrywood storage unit, only to ruin the effect with hurriedly fitted shelves at the end. If you expect a beautifully finished environment, accept now that it's your responsibility to keep those standards high.

this picture **At its simplest, the concept for a flexible home lies in creating multi-functional rooms. A sitting room may include a dining or study corner, or a bedroom boast a small interconnecting room, which may function alternately as a dressing room, baby's nursery, or home office.**

The best-planned homes happily adapt to the ebb and flow of life as years pass by. There may be the need to accommodate a growing family, perhaps, or to find room for an aged relative. If you're investing time and effort to achieve the perfect living space, then try to look five, even ten, years hence and make sure your property can anticipate upcoming demands. It's expensive and disruptive to move house continually. Far better to plan a space that can reinvent itself, or be elegantly and easily extended.

room to grow: the flexible home template

The most flexible home template is one that has a mix of well-proportioned, decent-sized rooms, with good natural lighting, plus several smaller ones. At ground level, large rooms may alternately be used as a sitting room, dining room, or a chill-out zone. At upper levels, there's the option of master bedroom, upstairs drawing room, or kids' playroom. Small rooms offer every option, from bedrooms, to walk-in wardrobe, dressing room or study. Provided each one is fitted with sufficient power points, overhead and task lighting, and storage (however minimal), as years pass they can swap functions with comparative ease. If finance permits, always buy a home with 'spare' rooms which you can grow into.

For those who prefer open-plan living, the answer is to pick a loft, lateral conversion of two flats, or an apartment that offers free-flowing spaces. Of course, bathrooms and kitchen will remain static. But then it's up to you to create one or two sitting spaces, family den or office as and when you need it, dictated by the furniture that's chosen and the way it is arranged. If you have a tall, thin property already, then removing part of the first floor and creating a double-height ground floor creates flexible living spaces, too.

If extra square footage is crucial, then look at your own property (or a possible new home) and consider its potential for expansion. Many period properties contain a loft, which is easily converted into an entire new floor of living space. Increasingly, there's also a vogue for digging out the basement of a house, to create room for a large kitchen. Both ideas constitute an investment, but will cost substantially less than moving house. If expansion is a long-term strategy, it's worth applying straight away for planning permission. If this is refused, then there's time to appeal. Just remember that many authorities require that work begins within a specified time period.

For some, it's more important to create day-to-day extra living space, so the main option is to create a ground-floor extension. Increasingly, the trend is to add a contemporary 'box' onto a period property, often with glass sliding doors leading onto a garden. Such an extension simultaneously creates more floor space, adds light and gives a modern slant to traditional living quarters.

opposite **If space permits, interconnecting living rooms like these provide the ideal template for today's fluid lifestyles. Furniture is easily cleared for parties, or a dining area reconfigured as a casual home office. In a family house, the area closest to the kitchen may change from play zone to family sitting room in later years.**

left **Don't underestimate the ability of small rooms to double up. If a study is eventually needed as a guest bedroom, a sitting room can still elegantly accommodate a desk.**

below **Spare space, from a room alcove to a landing, can be 'grown into' for a study or quiet corner as different lifestyle needs arise.**

Small rooms offer every option, from bedrooms to dressing room or study.

But it's not the only solution. Many older properties can be sympathetically extended to match the original building.

If finances allow, do try to complete the loft conversion or extension at the same time as any other major building work. This means pipes and wiring can be concealed prior to final decoration throughout, not to mention finding another location for the cold-water tank, which is normally housed in the loft. And a ground-floor extension will work seamlessly with an existing rear kitchen if a new floor links the two, rather than trying to add it on several years later.

This period home is dominated by vistas and muted sunlight. Its neutral colour palette, running to aubergine and eau-de-Nil, has been picked to play up tonal shifts from light to dark, while its simple original timber features are inspiration for bespoke joinery and honest, natural textures.

thoughts and plans case study

opposite **When a period home has beautiful bones, as this one has, the best advice is to work with them, restoring surfaces and sympathetically updating plumbing or lighting if required. If natural materials are already present, then use them as a springboard for a decorating palette.**

above **When several rooms interconnect on one level, a continuous floor is the single most unifying factor.**

right **Throw the emphasis onto a wonderful feature, such as a staircase, by paring down all surrounding furnishings.**

Architecturally speaking, here is a house that links together naturally. With its interconnected living spaces flowing off a central hall and stairwell, the space feels all of a piece. To the right of the hall is a drawing room. To the left, there is an *enfilade* of kitchen/dining room and a family sitting room. Upstairs, internal doors link master bedroom to a dressing room, and bathroom beyond. There's also privacy: rooms may be shut off by tall double doors.

With such excellent physical connections, the owners concentrated on planning colour, joinery, texture and furniture to shape the area. All, in turn, echo three key themes. First, the natural ebb and flow of sunlight as it passes into each room, and from one room to another. There's the strong visual character of the architectural features: timber floors and beams, panelled doors, period mouldings. Perhaps most importantly, there is a distinctive ambience – moody, yet tranquil – to be played up.

Colour choices are muted, yet surprisingly pretty. Along with fresh white and its partner, matt black, there are sombre greys, from charcoal to flannel, plus taupe and biscuit. These deep shades promote a calm atmosphere. But they've also been chosen to work with, not against, the naturally dark rooms, while the white highlights sunny areas such as the hall. Like an artist shading in pencil, they emphasize shadows and contours already there.

There's also a deliberate mix of tone throughout the house, to give the impression of moving from light to dark, then back again, and to emphasize the flow of light. In the bedroom, for example, walls are pale, with curtains in dark fabric. Pass into the dressing room, and one is plunged into the darkness of upholstered walls. Walk through to the bathroom, and all is white, light and bright. Yet the palette is lightened with frivolous accents: a scarlet lampshade in the dressing room, and in the

far left and left **Many decorative schemes use patterns as a common link, but throughout this house the theme is plain on plain. Emphasis is placed on key textures that are repeated from room to room: robust linens, wood floors, and rustic timber furniture.**

far left **It can be tricky to choose the right piece of furniture to sit in a central hall, midway between two rooms. The piece must be slimline, so as not to impede a view from one room to the next, and be in a colour that links with both. This stool works because it is low, and the aubergine is complementary to both schemes.**

left and above **Living rooms – dining, cooking and play areas – have sensibly been located in the naturally sunny part of the house. To emphasize the daylight, the paler spectrum shades have been picked from the palette: eau-de-Nil, neutral linen, and stripped pine for the shutters.**

hall, an aubergine stool. Because key neutrals are strong, it's possible to dip in and out of unusual shades without overbalancing the colour theme.

Existing architectural features loosely inspire the bespoke carpentry, but they are simple, so there's no need for slavish authenticity. Original panelled shutters and doors are mirrored in a new, free-standing headboard in the master bedroom. Less obviously, but equally dramatic, the simple geometry of the ceiling beams prompted plain joinery, from the flush door fronts in the kitchen and bathroom to the understated drawing-room fire surround.

Cleverly, the owners have also used the contrast of several natural textures – smooth versus rough, mottled versus plain – for a cohesive visual link.

this page **The ceiling beams are very dominant, so it made sense to let them dictate the theme in the master bedroom. The regular grid above has inspired the simple symmetry of identical** bedside tables and lamps. **The darkness of the ceiling beams also needs balancing out. The choice of grey wool blanket on the bed, and the deep grey drapes along the window wall, works perfectly.**

right **Much planning has gone into the traffic flow of this family home. A small room located just before the main hall has been assigned as a walk-in cloakroom. This means that arriving guests don't clutter up the hall, spoiling its dramatic impact.**

right, below **Every continuous theme needs a touch of contrast. A curly lamp base and round pouffe in the dressing room provide light relief from the prevailing cubed and contemporary furniture.**

It emphasizes the light and dark theme, and moulds ambience from room to room. So, while in the dressing room there's the sensual mix of wool, velvet and silk, in the bathroom there's the smooth contrast of marble and glass, and an upbeat mood. In the drawing room, the ambience changes once more, with cosy linen and wicker. The secret to combining so many textures, yet

retaining cohesion, lies in the timber floors, which seamlessly link every room.

Because of the vast scale of the rooms, emphasis naturally falls onto the silhouettes of key pieces of furniture. So the owners used cohesive shapes to link every room. Upholstered pieces are almost cubic in their simplicity, and similarly plain contours are echoed in the stone bath and the dining table. The added bonus? Any major piece could be moved from one room to another, and still look appropriate.

above **In a sunny room, the palette switches back to fresh whites, teamed with glass, to play up the daylight. Inspired by the grid of beams, an alcove is lined from floor to ceiling with open shelves.**

this page **In today's streamlined interiors, no one wants to look at sundry plumbing pipes or wiring snaking up a wall. But planning early isn't just about concealing the nuts and bolts of everyday services. It concerns getting taps, or lights, or an inset fireplace, into a user-friendly location for each room.**

bare essentials

Hard-working, practical details – from the flow of hot water and heating, to well-planned storage and robust surfaces – are the lifeblood of home. Seamlessly incorporated, they make  light work of daily living. But plan them methodically. Decisions taken singly must add up to one faultlessly functioning, harmonious home.

the flow of natural light

Sunlight pouring into a room is the most natural service we have. It illuminates and warms, not to mention subconsciously affects mood. So it's crucial to observe the flow of light in your property, and to get to know it. Assess its quality. Is it cool and northern, or do rooms have a southerly, sunny aspect? If you're not sure, then deliberately compare the positioning of your home in relation to where the sun rises and sets. Is there sunshine in the mornings, where do evening shadows fall? Consider your personality. Some people are deeply affected by lack of bright light, whereas others thrive on a moody chiaroscuro.

Extend your light survey to consider the number, size, style and location of windows throughout the home. Get out your rough floor plans and mark them up, adding notes about special features, such as dappled sunlight or light pooling on the floor, or whether certain times of the day are particularly ambient.

opposite **If there's a dominant view outside a window, build it into your scheme. Dense green foliage here calls for no window treatments at all.**

above right **Many stairwells are dark. A roof light not only floods light downwards, but introduces a crucial element of surprise as the visitor reaches the top.**

right **Once aware of the quality of light, it's easier to pick successful window treatments. In particular, shutters and Venetian blinds control sunshine and, with it, ambience.**

These observations will be crucial, first and foremost, to room planning. Busy daytime spaces should always be located in naturally sunny spots, whereas gloomier rooms make great evening sitting rooms or studies. The location of windows will also directly affect the success of a given furniture configuration. If there's a pretty Georgian sash, the window should be treated as a major focal point in the room, with chairs and tables arranged accordingly. In the case of French doors, the furniture must be planned to allow a direct exit and entry to the garden.

Remember that the quality, and quantity, of sunlight dramatically affects colour tone. Many decorators recommend using warm shades to counteract cool, northern light, or robust, vibrant hues to match a sunny room. But it can be more effective – and more interesting – to pick colour tones that deliberately play up natural shadows and highlights. Off-pastels, near-whites and neutrals are kinder and more subtle ways to emphasize a naturally sunny room, while muted greys, and deeps such as indigo or aubergine, will shape shady areas.

Also ask yourself how the flow of light will affect planned surfaces in each room. For example,

Busy daytime spaces should be located in naturally sunny spots, whereas gloomier rooms make great evening sitting rooms or studies.

Window styles will naturally dictate the most user-friendly furniture arrangement. *left* **A deep, sunny bay presents a neat alcove for a dining table, while** *above* **twin sashes inspire a symmetrical placing of furniture and accessories.**

opposite **Directing light from two sources looks particularly dramatic. In this new extension, sliding doors, as well as a skylight, illuminate a city house.**

honed, rather than glossy, granite will work most comfortably in a very sunny room. And a leather floor, nicely worn and scuffed, looks all the more effective in a shadowy interior.

In addition, the light-flow survey will highlight areas that could benefit from a new window. While not a venture to be undertaken lightly, the insertion of a single roof light – to direct sunshine right down into a stairwell – can dramatically enhance the look and mood of the whole property. Likewise, a new extension may be planned with floor-to-ceiling glass doors, or even completely composed of glass, to let sunshine flood across the entire floor level.

SERVICES CHECKLIST

- Get a professional to check wiring and plumbing. If it needs overhauling, is the budget available?

- Are any rooms consistently chilly or too hot? Do any radiators break up the run of a wall/spoil a window?

- Does the style of radiators jar? Is underfloor or grille heating an option?

- Do you want the ambience of an open or faux gas fire?

- Does the lighting work well for you? Are there enough task lights? In the right places? Which rooms need extra lighting, to improve ambience or drama?

- Does the plumbing work well? Is the tank big enough to cope with several bathrooms?

- Is feeble water pressure a problem, or should you add a water pump to improve water flow?

- Will TV/hi-fi/computer go on show, or be concealed?

this page **Properly planned, an inset gas-effect fire can become an integral part of the architecture. Here, the hearthstone extends to one side to form a convenient bench.**

above right **Don't hesitate to replace ugly radiators with modern or attractive Victorian-style models. Then they become a decorative feature, rather than something to disguise.**

centre left **In small flats or modern homes, floor grille heating is discreet, and doesn't take up valuable wall space.**

centre right **Consider ways to conceal air-conditioning or heating grilles within new joinery. Here, they all but disappear into the deep windowsill.**

below right **Match the style of radiators to your décor. This one blends with the curtain folds, whereas flat panel versions are good with plain painted walls.**

Think of the pleasures of a good hotel, where plumbing is plentiful, lighting is ambient and (if you're lucky) there's music in the bathroom. Then apply this spoil-me principle to your home. Does everything work this perfectly? If not, list what you'd like to change, then cost it up with a professional. For sure, most of us don't have hotel-size budgets. But the relatively minor investment required for an electrician to wall-mount lights by your bed, or even the more significant cost of replacing a too-small hot-water tank, will reap benefits later on.

immaculate services

Whether revamping a wreck or building from scratch, now's the time to review the major issues, such as rewiring or upgrading a boiler, because there will be inevitable disruption. But it's also your chance to consider ultra-efficient heating options, or the installation of more complex lighting. So think back to your ultimate decorative vision. Is a minimalist environment important? Then consider invisible underfloor heating, discreet heating grilles or flat panel radiators. Is a high-tech look crucial? What about fibre-optic lighting beneath a kitchen worktop, or a hall dramatically washed with low-voltage spots?

Sometimes, services work perfectly efficiently, but – especially in older buildings – aren't in the right places for today's lifestyle. In particular, we demand more from our lighting. These days, a solo pendant light and plug-in lamp aren't enough for home socializing and quiet work. First keep in mind that every room needs general illumination, task lamps, and mood lighting. Then refer back to your lifestyle notes, and check on any specific needs, such as a wall-mounted office light (so it doesn't topple off the desk) or dimmer switches (to give every room much-needed tranquillity). Only when you know exactly what you're after (it can help to sketch out lighting plans for each room) should you brief an electrician and gather quotes.

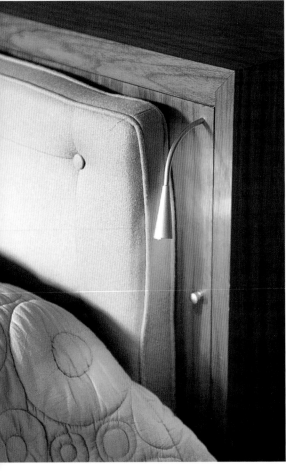

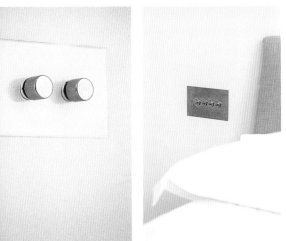

left and above **Be very specific as to what each task light is for, as this will affect its design. A solo bedside light can afford to be this tiny, whereas in the dining room the adjustable overhead lights need to be large enough to illuminate the entire table.**

above right **If there's art to highlight, plan dramatic lights as well as basic lighting. Ceiling-mounted spots are adaptable, as they can be reangled if a display is rearranged.**

left **Little details, like identical light switches in every room, make for a cohesive interior. Pick a finish to match other detailing, such as chrome to blend with taps, or brushed stainless steel to match a splashback.**

The best-planned services concern good looks, as well as faultless functioning. At its most basic level, that means wires and cables completely concealed behind walls and floors. So accept that even minor interventions will require a touch of redecoration. Alternatively, if there's no chance of hiding wires or plumbing in the fabric of the building, can a piece of built-in furniture screen them? Inset open shelves (designed to pull out for essential maintenance) might fill in a cavity needed to house an en suite bathroom water pump, or a purpose-built cabinet may conceal the necessary technology to feed wall-to-wall

The best-planned services concern good looks, as well as faultless functioning.

this picture and right
To create an imposing hall, it can be no more expensive to install spectacular staircase lights or wall-washing spots than it is to hang a designer wallpaper. So weigh up your priorities. To get ideas, look at books on contemporary architecture or interiors magazines, then research available fittings. You needn't spend a fortune, provided the planning is sound and electrical work professional.

below, left and right **For a cohesive look, use just a few light styles through the house. Pick modern, discreet fittings for halls and ceilings, plus more decorative shades for wall-mounted lights in the bedroom or sitting room.**

this picture **A shower enclosure is infinitely more sophisticated if pared down to barely more than an overhead shower rose. But once tiling is complete, there's no chance to make changes, so ensure that the wall controls are at the correct height. If a false ceiling is installed overhead to conceal pipework, then consider the inclusion of feature lighting at the same time.**

right, below **A user-friendly washroom must have fittings at the correct height, as well as neat storage. So think through your showering needs. This one has been tiled to include an inset soap shelf, as well as a separate hair-washing hose.**

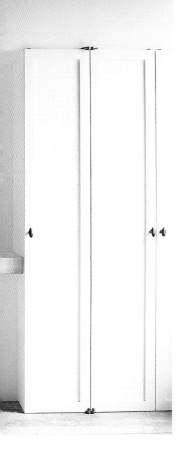

Don't overlook smaller details, such as supplying sufficient electrical sockets, phone points, and light switches. List what you use in a space.

music around the house. If it's conventional radiators that offend your eye, then consider investing in prettier versions, or sleek designer ones. Good radiators can make a dramatic difference to a room.

Don't overlook smaller details, such as supplying sufficient electrical sockets, phone points, and light switches. Provided there is already one socket available, it's a minor job for an electrician to add more. So take the time to list what items you'll use in a given space (an iron, hairdryer, bedside light, TV, radio are just for starters in a bedroom). And remember the hall and landings. There should be plugs for the Hoover, and staggered light switches, so you can extinguish hall lights and still be illuminated on the way up to bed.

above **Today's vogue for wall-mounted taps means it's essential to conceal plumbing in the wall. Think carefully about tap height in relation to the basin. Too low, for example, and you can't easily splash water upwards. If your choice of modern taps means the fitting of a water pump, built-in cupboards in the bathroom are a discreet way to hide it.**

right **For music fans, installing ceiling or wall speakers in every room is a must. Many specialist home entertainment companies can offer this service, often with extras such as centralized computer, lighting and media systems.**

cohesive architectural detailing

Visit any professionally designed interior, and it is odds-on that architectural detailing will be cohesive. There will be identical door handles, open shelves all of one thickness, and uniform skirting heights, to mention a few. We may not actively notice these, but will subconsciously register a sense of harmony. That's because well-conceived detailing packs a powerful decorative punch. Be it simple or elaborate, it links spaces effectively and provides vital finishing touches to the architecture. So give your property due attention. Work out what features are original: do they still look good? Have no qualms about whipping out later additions that don't look right. Better to start with a clean slate, and impose sleek detailing, than put up with a muddle of styles.

In a period property that has retained its pretty features, from deep skirtings to panelled doors, there may be little cosmetic work to do. It's worth the effort of replacing, say, stray modern doors, or a Seventies brick fire surround. Don't get hung up on period details: unless your property is listed, getting features right is more about a visual tidying up than textbook authenticity. If the process of knocking two rooms together has ruined original cornice work, then get a plaster specialist to copy

opposite **Dominant** architectural features such as windows are a rich source for joinery themes. *left* **Here, a glass and wood screen has been inspired by the geometric grid of the ceiling beams, while** *right* metal windows were the starting point for glass-fronted kitchen cupboards.

this page **Panelling is a particularly versatile feature. It can be repeated from room to room, to** create a unified whole throughout a property. Yet its regular pattern can also be echoed in little, with square motifs appearing in a rug, upholstery textile or even picture frames.

left **Sometimes built-in cupboards on either side of a fire surround can destroy its decorative impact. Far better, then, to let a plain panelled mantelpiece be the starting point for the style of the cupboard doors.**

this picture **Similarly, don't let a fireplace dominate a pretty wall of panelling. Choose a surround that blends with it instead.**

Don't get hung up on period details: getting features right is more a visual tidying up than textbook authenticity.

opposite **It can be fun to play with a given detail, even repeating the pattern with well-chosen furniture. Here, tongue-and-groove joinery is inspired by the parallel lines of the beams above, echoed again in the spindles of the Windsor chair.**

right **You may need to adapt a detail, and be prepared to scale it up or down. This cupboard was copied from the existing panelled door, then cheekily elongated to give an Alice in Wonderland feel to the room.**

the existing pattern. It won't be cheap, but the resulting seamless link will be worth it.

In a modern home, you can experiment with contemporary detailing. This might be as simple as having no skirtings or adding plain, boxy stone fire surrounds. If there's more substantial building work in progress, it may mean including shadow gaps at top and bottom of walls, or identical inset shelving that repeats in every room. The key factor is to pick your theme, then stick faithfully to it.

Given our current obsession with the modern, sometimes it's necessary to reconcile two

left **Great architectural detailing also concerns scale. Here, a modern stone fire surround blends with traditional panelling above. It works because the fireplace width perfectly balances the chunky vertical panels. To get proportions right, sketch to-scale drawings before you commission a new surround or panels.**

below **Where old and new details join, as with this period fireplace and flush doors, use a single item as a visual link. The boxy chair sits well with the modern doors. Yet its classically simple lines look just as good with the period marble surround.**

contrasting styles. The answer is to make the collision look deliberate. Filling the room with a mix of period and modern furniture helps with the transition. So, too, does colour uniformity: a traditional grey slate floor with an industrial stainless-steel kitchen work bench, say, or an all-white bathroom that combines ultra-modern fittings with traditional marble worktops.

If a space has only a few interesting features, then seize on them as inspiration for bespoke joinery, or even the theme for a new kitchen. A carpenter can scale up cupboard doors to match an original panelled wall, or mirror the grid of a beamed ceiling in radiator covers. Don't limit the theme to one room. Identical cupboard doors, open shelves or panelling all link a space together.

Smaller details, such as door handles and window fittings, are just as vital. You can go ultra-simple, with touch-catch flush doors, or decorative, with handles shaped as leaves or pebbles. Use large versions on doors, scaled-down ones on cupboards. If there's an antique version, investigate getting it copied. If handles are metal, try to match them to light switches and plug covers.

ARCHITECTURAL DETAILS CHECKLIST

- Locate your favourite architectural details. Sketch or imagine how they may be reinterpreted in new ways around the house.

- Look for interesting patterns, such as the criss-cross of a parquet floor, which may be echoed in upholstery or rugs.

- Be a perfectionist: are all details in similar styles/materials?

If a space has interesting features, then seize on them as inspiration for bespoke joinery. Don't limit the theme to one room.

this page **Door handles are frequently overlooked in the decorating process, yet are just as vital a link as colour, or surfaces. Do your research to find good ones. Look beyond department stores, and seek out specialist retailers. Some handles can be very expensive, and you may be buying many. But it is worth the investment: if you can't alter all your cupboard doors to match, for example, paint them the same colour, and add identical handles. The effect will be almost as striking. Try to find handles that come in several different sizes, so you can add mini ones to wardrobes or use them to customize chests of drawers, and add an extra-large one to the front or back door. And consider touch. Architects set as much store by the feel of a door handle as they do by its looks.**

this page **Look to existing architectural features to spark design ideas, so storage blends seamlessly with the whole room. These tall inset display shelves, for example, echo the lines and lofty dimensions of the nearby archway. Plenty of space between shelves, plus minimal detailing, puts the artefacts centre stage.**

storage and space savers

Plentiful and well-planned storage is the secret to a hard-working home. Cupboards hide everyday chaos, so make for a streamlined interior. And if there's a place for everything, we feel peaceful. Start by taking an inventory of how well your current storage works. It's never too late to add more, but the earlier you plan, the more imaginative and tailor-made the solutions can be.

First it's vital to list everything that needs house room. Do this by category, rather than room by room, as it prompts a centralized approach to storage: all vases in the utility room, say, or all photos in the study. Also, divide things into 'active' storage – articles used on a daily/weekly basis – and 'passive' storage, like picnic kit. These can go in less accessible cupboards.

Also plan the type of storage. The average home requires a good mix of wardrobes, bookshelves, open shelves and general

left **Slim built-in or wall-hung furniture not only looks neat, but contributes to a streamlined mood. Although quite deep, this cupboard looks wafer thin because it has been inset into a wall between hall and dining room, cleverly accessed by doors on both sides.**

this picture **Materials or colours behind inset shelves make powerful linking tools. The walnut used here is repeated for a variety of storage options around the home.**

Storage with a strong decorative theme is the ultimate visual unifier. It might be as simple as plumping for thick, open MDF shelves throughout.

cupboards, as well as task-specific storage, like a bathroom cabinet. So tweak the list to match your lifestyle. If clothes are important, measure hangers and count shoes. If books and CDs are plentiful, tailor-make a system to grow with the collection.

Next, survey every square metre at home. Identify the obvious areas that can be filled with built-in cupboards (under the stairs or fireplace alcoves). Then think creatively. Could you 'steal' a section of wall in a bedroom for a run of cupboards, build

left **When planning an entire wall of shelves, a multi-tasking mix is best. Here, the combination of open bookshelves and deeper cabinets beneath not only provides a useful display surface between the two, but the chance for an impromptu desk area. A block of shelves can be very dominating visually, so plan it alongside furniture and accessories. This simple, yet modern cabinet blends well with the retro furniture and piece of contemporary art.**

above right **Coming to early conclusions about what you need from your home prompts useful space-saving solutions. Here, a new half partition wall was designed with inset shelves and a desktop, to provide a quiet study spot.**

right **An elegant storage system can be planned as the major focus in a room. Here, the symmetrical theme is played up with the careful placing of armchairs, and the neat arrangement of books.**

above **In open-plan zones, the partition between areas can be planned to incorporate lots of seamless storage. This one has open bookshelves on the sitting-room side, plus a recess for the TV in the bedroom behind. Flush floor-to-ceiling doors at the sides conceal yet more cupboards.**

around a door, or add bookshelves to a load-bearing column in an open-plan space? If building work is planned, there's more potential. Think of it as weaving storage into the fabric of the house. A plasterboard wall can be built with a cavity behind, into which inset shelves can be sunk. Or consider a cupboard that straddles a section of wall, and is accessed from either side.

Built-in furniture is the fastest route to bespoke storage. Don't be afraid to be very specific on depth, distance between shelves and so on. This is your home, so make it fit like a glove. If a room's use is likely to change over time, pick adaptable fittings, such as multi-adjustable shelves.

It's distinctive, and fun, to devise some storage around a specific function. The TV may be sunk into an aperture in a false wall (with or without sliding doors to conceal it), bookshelves planned with pull-out racks for magazines or cupboards built beneath a platform bed. The more focused you are on storage function, the easier it is to plan the extra details that elevate shelves from utility to design statement. For example, add inset lighting to deep display shelves, or insert floor-level niches beneath a built-in bench.

Free-standing and occasional wall-mounted furniture can also be tailor-made. The key is to sweep away existing internal fittings that aren't working, and replace with what does. The narrow shelves in a sitting-room sideboard may be removed, to allow you to stack the workings for the DVD and stereo, or you can refit a wardrobe with different-sized wire baskets and hooks, more user-friendly than a single hanging rail. High street stores offer a wonderful selection of cupboard organizer options.

The beauty of rethinking storage across the whole home is that you can take a logical, problem-solving approach to it. By inserting inset shelves into unexpected cavities, the majority of open wall spaces are reserved for attention-grabbing art

this page **The beauty of bespoke storage is that it can be multi-functional. In this modern house, a low bench combines impromptu seating, plus room below for magazines in baskets.**

opposite left **An MDF cube, painted to match the walls, provides a dramatic yet streamlined way to contain the TV.**

opposite right **Attic rooms, with sloping ceilings, offer plenty of potential for storage, either in cupboard form or as more design-conscious inset shelving. Source storage baskets first, then make shelves to fit them.**

or furniture. By lining one kitchen wall with floor-to-ceiling cupboards, there's less clutter in the hall. Often radical solutions come from thinking big scale. Could a cellar or utility room be filled with cupboards and racks, to become the storage nerve centre of the home, giving a streamlined look elsewhere? What about a box bedroom, or a slice of a larger room, which may be converted into a walk-in wardrobe, a link between bedroom and en suite bathroom?

Storage with a strong decorative theme is the ultimate visual unifier. It might be something as simple as plumping for thick, open MDF shelves throughout. Or you might choose a common material (from utility plywood to oak veneer), to be used on wardrobe doors, display shelves and a purpose-built TV cabinet. This is a perfect way to unify existing storage, if you can't start entirely from scratch. New cupboard doors, on original carcasses, will link every room.

above left **A small bedroom next to the master bedroom can be transformed into a dressing room. By fitting it with user-friendly open rails, shelves and a big mirror, the main sleeping space remains tranquil, free from overpowering wardrobes.**

right **Consider the dimensions of a bedroom and adjacent en suite bathroom. Can a narrow area be shaved off one, then enclosed with new partition walls, to create a walk-in wardrobe? Here, open shelves and hanging rails, either side of the linking doorway, give his and hers clothes storage.**

left and below left **Perfectly planned storage should also include quick-access solutions. A row of hooks can be useful in many places, from obvious locations like a hall, to the bedroom or bathroom, when a quick tidy-up or clothes change is required. Open shelves in a bathroom are a great solution for laundry or towels. But for a truly harmonious mood, keep them fastidiously tidy.**

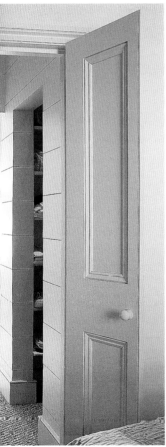

this picture **If there's a spare wall, or a cavity beneath the stairs, fill it with a bank of floor-to-ceiling cupboards to keep other rooms clutter free. Plan the inside carefully, with shelves in a variety of heights, and baskets or wire drawers to keep things in order. Add at least one hanging rail, for storing out of season clothes, or coats.**

STORAGE CHECKLIST

- How well does the existing storage work? What currently doesn't have a home?

- What's your storage 'personality'? Closed doors or open shelves? Built-in or free-standing?

- Is there sports equipment/collections for display/lots of shoes that need specialized storage?

- What areas can be exploited to create new storage?

- How much day-to-day storage is needed, and what can be stored in less accessible areas?

- Can any rooms/parts of a room be devoted to storage, such as a walk-in cloakroom?

- Think of your favourite styles (plain or moulded shelves, flush or panelled doors) and potential materials (wood, glass, MDF, stainless steel).

opposite **A gentle painted wall finish makes an excellent, yet subtle, linking surface, as appropriate in a bedroom as in a drawing room. Precisely because the colours will be mixed by hand to suit, it can be varied tonally from one room to another; lightened to cope with a bright room, darkened to promote a moody interior.**

linking surfaces

The focus of decorating has changed. When once we grappled with paints and fabrics, now the vogue for hard floors and contemporary surfaces makes choices wider, and a whole lot trickier to pull together. But get the mix right, and great surfaces can forge a dynamic link throughout your home.

Sleek surfaces are the mood of the moment. Hard floors have soared in popularity, in every form from solid timber and wood laminates, to rubber, stone, or leather. Kitchens and bathrooms are more modern and minimalist, so traditional ceramic-tiled splashbacks have been ousted in favour of stainless steel, sandblasted glass or laminates. And it's a short design hop to the increasing vogue for using dramatic textures on walls: a plaster finish, say, or a feature wall in grained wood veneer.

It's fun to experiment, but first address the practicalities. It's crucial to explore the potential of

any given surface, so you know the best places to use it, and where to avoid it. There's no point picking limestone for floors and matching shower enclosure, only to discover that its thickness is too heavy to line the walls. So do your research with specialist shops and suppliers. Ask about a material's suitability for wall-mounting, its water resistance if used as a bath panel or kitchen splashback, and its longevity. Will it age gracefully? Will it need constant cleaning to look good?

Think of budget. The cost of many hardwood or stone surfaces runs from moderate to sky's the

this page **If hard surfaces at home are limited solely to the bathrooms and kitchen, consider dovetailing them all, so the sleek, functioning rooms feel of a piece. Pick surfaces that will look appropriate in either setting. These simple brick-style white tiles are stylish and crisp in the kitchen, and look equally fresh in the shower room.**

When it comes to picking surfaces, do so in the context of the whole home. Using a different decorative surface in each room may look confused.

limit, so return to your costings and see whether you need to adjust a scheme to include lesser amounts. A little of a beautiful surface can go a long way. A marble vanity unit worktop in the bathroom can look just as pretty as a floor-to-ceiling version.

When it comes to picking surfaces, do so in the context of the whole home. Using a different decorative surface in each room runs the risk of a confused look as you travel through the house: stainless steel and glass in the kitchen, timbers in the bedroom,

a choice of limestone in the bathroom. Far easier on the eye, on the other hand, would be a combination of a single timber and limestone, with sandblasted glass and stainless steel for detailing (on cupboards or doors). It's also easier on the purse, as buying one or two choice surfaces in quantity can be cheaper than many smaller cuts of stone.

After honing down favourites, decide now whether you'll stick to one linking surface, or use a palette of several. In its simplest form, a unifying hard surface might be a timber floor that runs across the ground floor. Or it may be the decision to choose polished plaster walls throughout, or oak-panelled storage everywhere. If there is to be only one dominant surface, it's crucial to pick a neutral one, which can blend with a variety of shades or patterns in different rooms. It must be multi functional, able to cope with hard traffic in the hall, water in the bathroom and so on.

Another option is to play with 'families' of surfaces. Glass might be a theme, used as modern glass stair treads, an illuminated glass bath panel,

right **In compact areas such as this bathroom, there's a particularly dramatic and unifying effect to be had by using identical timber for floor and a portion of wall.**

below left and right **In adjoining rooms, such as a bedroom and en suite, surface links may be very subtle. Here, the timber of the headboard is echoed in the honey tones of the wood vanity top. In a linked kitchen/dining room, an identical stone worktop might be used for units and table too.**

this page **Look out for
surfaces such as tongue-and-
groove panelling, which are
versatile enough to use as
interior and exterior detailing
on a house, and throughout
many different rooms. The
design is simple, so it looks
appropriate in a kitchen,
bathroom, landing or
bedroom. It can be painted
in an identical shade
throughout, or used as a
subtler link, varying from
neutrals to definite colours.
It even looks good with a
variety of furniture styles,
from contemporary to very
traditional. In a property
where there are many doors,
and glimpses from room to
room, it can be a particularly
useful tool, ironing out
architectural dissimilarities,
and forging a cohesive whole.**

opposite **The simple,
geometric lines of squared
panelling, or tongue-and-
groove, make a good basis for
playing with different scales.
For example, the proportions
of squares may be adapted
for a small bedroom, then
over-scaled for a grand
drawing room, meanwhile
retaining a strong visual link
around the house. In the
same vein, the broad lines
of the tongue-and-groove
panelling, shown here, are
used to ring the changes.
In the kitchen, it's used
vertically, and in the
bathroom, fixed horizontally,
to give a more contemporary
twist. Don't overlook the fun
to be had from merging
patterns on surfaces.
Here, there's a successful
integration of stripes, from
the tongue-and-groove and
board floor, to the panelled
settle and column radiator.**

and sandblasted glass bedroom wardrobe doors. In more traditional homes, slate may be repeated as floor tiles, on the kitchen work surfaces, and to line the shower. For the nervous, a selection of timbers makes a good start, as it's mellow to look at and easy to live with even in large quantities.

For more dramatic looks, opt for a limited palette of surfaces that introduce a touch of contrast. This might be textural (the roughness of plywood versus smooth glass), or tonal (rich macassar ebony teamed with pale granite). Then you can have fun ringing the changes from room to room, using key materials in varying quantities. Don't make too many rules, and don't assume that every surface in the palette must be used each time. It's always useful to include one or two blander surfaces (such as concrete or pale oak) to act as a foil to the more dramatic options.

Plan for physical links as one surface finishes and the next starts, as often the contrast between two hard surfaces is more striking than conventional painted wall meets timber floor. In modern properties, a shadow gap between the base of the wall and floor gives visual breathing space. Or have a low splashback in the same timber or stone as a kitchen worktop. Pay particular attention to the junction of different floor surfaces. In an open-plan area, this can be used to advantage, actively delineating various activity zones. But also consider subtly dropping a floor level as surfaces change, or choosing two contrasting floor surfaces, to make the switch look dramatic and deliberate.

opposite As well as formal fabric types, you can group materials more loosely according to texture. This bedroom combines a touchy-feely mix of leather, cashmere, and linen. Links here are extended to include a combination of soft materials, such as a leather rug and chest of drawers.

below Find clues for appropriate fabrics by referring back to the 'bones' of the building. This bedroom, which mixes linen with leather, was inspired by the raw quality of the beams.

With today's emphasis on plain-coloured, textural fabrics, rather than splashy patterns, choosing materials that subtly weave around the house should become second nature. For the minimally minded, a cotton weave, in three neutral tones (light to dark), is all that's needed to dress windows and upholstery. For the rest of us, it's fun to lace simple choices with the occasional twist: a great pattern or unusual fabrics.

linking fabrics

Traditionally, the practice of linking fabrics has been restricted to individual rooms: matching flowered chintz to a printed linen, or damask and silk stripes. Yet, for a truly cohesive look, it's important to plan schemes in the context of the whole home, so that key textures or patterns repeat from room to room.

At the simplest level, similar materials can be used to draw together an interior that is high on hard surfaces, but needs softening with fabric. Plain curtains or roman blinds, all identical, can be wonderfully unifying. So, too, can the same slip covers in every room: white cotton, say, or ticking.

For more elaborate schemes, it's up to you how tight, or loose, the links are. If the overall look is simple, then source a versatile upholstery- and curtain-weight linen union, available in several complementary shades, and make it the core textile. It can be used for upholstery, window treatments, and cushions, with variations on colour, or trimmings, to give individuality in each room. What matters most is that it forms a visual (and sensual) link from one room to the next.

For more sophisticated looks, and to give extra scope for fresh twists in each room, gather several textures (perhaps a wool weave, two cottons and a silk). There's plenty of potential here for varying moods – silk for an elegant sitting room, comforting wool upholstery in the dining room – but, provided the colour palette stays consistent, a consistency of texture remains. Look out for fabric collections with a choice of weaves, but all in one tone.

above left **For added impact, use lampshades, cushions or throws in similar textures, to build on the look of a curtain fabric. Scour high-street stores for these, or make your own from leftover upholstery material.**

above right **There is drama to be gained from using a fabric as matching headboard and upholstery material. The effect is simple, yet seamless.**

left **In an open-plan space, where windows are glimpsed from different zones throughout, it makes sense to keep curtains or blinds simple, and all in one material.**

Weave in other textiles (a little pattern here, a textural contrast there) to individualize rooms.

If it's difficult to work out which fabrics will suit a variety of rooms, prepare a sample board with swatches. Don't plan room by room. Instead, get a large sheet of card, sketch out every room on a particular floor, then start to assemble fabrics. You will soon see if a grey denim upholstery, or cream linen curtains, will work well throughout. Then

this page **The more interconnected the series of rooms, the more tightly planned the fabric links should be. In this apartment, the drawing room, bedroom and bathroom all have a unique flavour. Yet each room has been subtly drawn together, using a key fabric.** *above and far right* **The pretty eau-de-Nil linen appears as scatter cushions in the drawing room, and in the bedroom as cushions, chair upholstery and a cover.** *right* **Teamed with a water-resistant backing, it even reappears as an elegant shower curtain in the bathroom.**

this picture, right above and below **Patterned fabric can dramatically soften a modern look in a space composed of hard surfaces. Curtains would look too conventional, but upholstered double doors take a successful midline. The linen background teams with the concrete surfaces, and the suede of the cushions appears on the desktop next door.**

weave in other textiles (a little pattern here, a textural contrast there) to individualize rooms. If you can transfer a cushion, or piece of upholstery, from one room to another, and the fabrics still sit happily together, then your schemes will work.

Certain materials, which straddle the boundary between hard surfaces and soft fabrics, can be used very imaginatively. Hessian, for example, will look dramatic on a hall wall, and can then be subtly repeated on a bedhead. Leather, faux suede, and wool felt are also good options. All can be used as walling, tabletop surface, or to seamlessly cover panelled or flush wardrobe doors.

above **Where hard surfaces predominate, tread carefully when adding soft materials, to avoid a startling contrast. Stick to tight upholstery, and keep cushion covers plain. Using fabric on a door makes a subtle, but distinctive link between the two. Here, the contrast door stripes not only echo the suede cushions, but also the geometric lines of the stepped floor levels and low concrete bench.**

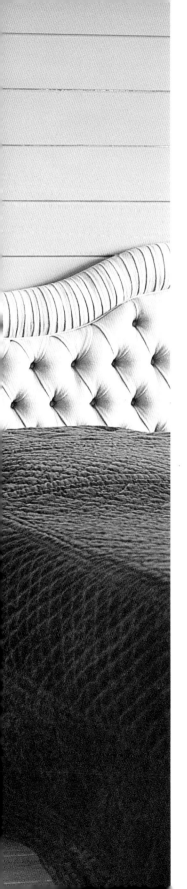

Consider decorating, and we automatically think of colour. It's the fastest way to personalize an interior, introduce new moods, or give shape to uninspired architecture. Yet properly planned, it's also the single most important tool for forging a cohesive look. So plan a working palette to link every room.

linking colours

When decorating from scratch, there's unbearable pressure to dream up different schemes for each room. The process of mixing and matching is tricky in itself, but there's also the risk of creating an interior with too many 'personalities', not to mention jarring glimpses of myriad colours from one room to another. No wonder many of us choose white as the easy option.

By contrast, a home feels calmer if colours blend smoothly throughout the whole interior. A carefully chosen palette (from three to six shades) can be reworked in varying tones and quantities, in every room. And the benefits are manifold. There's a harmonious mood because spaces are linked by colour. There's adaptability, because toning decorative items can sit just as happily in several different rooms. And one palette means shopping for accessories is a breeze.

The core palette will depend not just on the colours you personally find uplifting, but how light or dark the property is, whether the planned mood is to be cosy or tranquil, and if the desired decorative effect is dramatic or soothing. Alongside the two or three key colours, there must be a contrast, deeper tone, one neutral and a brighter,

left **One mid-toned wall shade can link an entire home. Here, it's moody and calm, teamed with neutral upholstery.**

below **Dark skirtings, mouldings, and window frames create discreet yet harmonious links.**

accent shade. Don't forget to try potential colours against planned hard surfaces. Not every natural material like wood or stone looks 'neutral'; many have a definite colour.

Next, armed with watercolours or colouring pencils, sketch each room and fill in blocks of planned colour on walls, upholstery and floors. You don't have to be artistic to do this, and it doesn't matter if paints are approximations of the shades. This exercise allows you to lay sketches all together on the floor, see whether the balance of light and dark tones feels comfortable, if individual room colours look good with the scheme for the hall, or where a particular space needs accent shades.

Colour linking can be as subtle as you wish. The simplest device is to paint walls identically throughout, with fresh key shades introduced in furnishings. A double-aspect room may be painted in the same colour, but using a pale tone for the shadier rear aspect, and a stronger one at the front. Sweeps of a deeper shade may dominate ground-floor walls, balanced with pale floors, only to be reversed upstairs with white walls and dark floors. Coloured woodwork,

this page **In a modern home, individual sections of painted wall are often the simplest and most appropriate way to introduce colour. Yet it can be distracting to use too many contrasting, vibrant shades. The most successful (and dramatic) device for linking just a couple is to choose an abstract motif. Then it can, as here, be reworked in two colours, teamed with white. A target design, simple stripes, or large dots all work effectively. Here, the yellow in the centre of the target, on the corridor wall, is just a taster of the sunny yellow kitchen around the corner. Then the target design is repeated, this time in fresh white.**

rather than conventional white, also forges a single, but firm link.

For the brave, colour is a dramatic tool. For example, an interior might sport a drawing room with white walls, aubergine panel, and charcoal upholstery, with scarlet cushions. In the kitchen, cabinets may be scarlet gloss laminate, with grey slate floor and white walls. In the hall beyond, walls may be moody charcoal, with a stunning red chandelier.

above left **For white-walls-only fans, furnishings are the perfect vehicle for co-ordinating colour. Here, black velvet upholstery and pale grey curtains and bedcover create a sophisticated, yet harmonious bedroom.**

below left **When rooms interconnect, instead of matching wall colours, experiment with tonal shifts between them.**

this picture **Built-in storage blends in more easily painted the same tone as walls, rather than white.**

COLOUR CHECKLIST

- Which colours do you like best? Do you prefer neutrals, pastels, shades of white, deeps or bright colours?

- Are you a one-colour person, or would you rather have a decent mix of shades?

- Is the space open-plan? Can colour be used to unify spaces, or alternatively to delineate active or peaceful zones?

- Look at your planned hard surfaces: do they tone well or fight with potential colours?

- How important is pattern? One strong design can be the core to a working palette throughout a home.

A carefully chosen palette can be reworked in varying tones and quantities, in every room.

this page and opposite
One zany, colourful pattern can form the core of a single scheme. In this double-height space with a mezzanine floor, the bright wallpaper runs vertically throughout. A clever mix of exact colour matches, plus some tonal adjustments, have been extracted from it and used in varying amounts, to create different moods in each area. Sage and dark woods mark out the tranquil bathroom space, while a strong yellow delineates the main wall of the living room. Fabric details link in, too. Cushion edges are in egg yolk, and the brown sofa upholstery balances the dark woods upstairs.

bare essentials case study

A strong and cohesive style envelops this family house, from front door to top floor. With a select mix of natural hard materials, from limestone to walnut, and soft textiles, from silk to retro prints, colours are muted, but classic-contemporary furniture makes the space practical and funky.

left and above right and left **Surfaces go a long way to creating visual harmony, but uniformity of furniture styles helps, too. The spindly legged silhouette of Eames dining chairs is echoed in the kitchen bar stools. Matching furniture to built-in features also reinforces style. Here, the slab-style dining table matches the kitchen work surface.**

above right and left **In an open-plan space where floor levels change, it can be more dramatic to vary flooring, from light to dark, then back again as the level drops further.**

Walk through this home and what strikes first is its satisfying uniformity of style. Look again, and each room has distinctive features. In the sitting room, tones are pale and sophisticated, with white Knoll sofas and Fifties-style textiles. In the kitchen, the mood is family-friendly, with robust walnut floors and stools. Such a confident mix is no easy feat.

So what's the secret to making it hang together so well? The key lies in a cleverly restricted mix of surfaces and colours, which reappear around the

left **Think not just of the scale, but of the height of furniture in an open-plan space. Despite changing floor levels, the kitchen and formal seating area feel cohesive, because the eye travels easily from low stools to low cabinet beyond.**

below left **The ultimate well-planned storage: with no trailing wires, the TV and stereo disappear into walnut units.**

right **Choose a silhouette for your space, and stick to it. The boxy sofas echo the modern fireplace, which repeats the square aperture connecting sitting area to kitchen.**

The hard surfaces were picked to define the living space, and give it an architectural character that it lacked before.

house. All walls and ceilings are polished plaster, and all joinery is rich, solid walnut. The staircase is concrete, as is the kitchen worktop. Flooring is in pale limestone slabs. The hard surfaces were picked to define the living space, and give it an architectural character that it lacked before. They ebb and flow deliberately, moving from pale to dark, textured to smooth, and back.

And it's because the surfaces mix is unusual – grown-up walnut with trendy concrete – that they can be teamed with a broad range of soft furnishings and create individual looks. In the bedroom are chic olive greens and crunchy silks, and in the kitchen, black leather and frosted glass; but the key elements remain the same.

left **In a hall that offers vistas to rooms and levels beyond, it's even more essential that materials cohere. But also consider the shapes and silhouettes created by architectural features. This view is carefully conceived, mixing rectangles, vertical and horizontal, with the surprise of a modern staircase twisting through the centre.**

right, main picture **The floor area of the master bedroom has been expertly reworked to incorporate plentiful wardrobes. They've been designed to look good, and be accessible from the bedroom side, as well as enclosing a private dressing area, and forming a 'corridor' to the study beyond. The wardrobes aren't full height, so the room doesn't feel hemmed in. The centrally placed bed guarantees easy routes from study to landing, and from en suite bathroom to wardrobes.**

above far right **A sliding door in sandblasted glass seamlessly links en suite bathroom to bedroom. Not only does it assure privacy, but allows light to flow between the rooms.**

below far right **Shapes and textures in the bathroom repeat themes elsewhere. A slatted Venetian blind echoes the grille style of the gantry, in both dining room and bedroom, and the mirror and vanity unit are finished in walnut.**

The well-planned layout creates the perfect balance between shared and private zones. The double-height hall promotes active circulation, offering twin entrances to the ground floor, or leading upstairs. While living areas are open-plan, each activity area is subtly delineated, with a stepped floor leading from dining room to kitchen, then to the sitting zone. In neat contrast, upstairs is a series of more intimate, linked rooms. With sliding doors between master bed and bath, and wardrobes partitioning dressing room and study, privacy is assured.

It's because the surfaces mix is unusual — grown-up walnut with trendy concrete — that they can be teamed with a broad range of soft furnishings for individual looks.

opposite **With moveable screens and slim partition walls, an open-plan space provides the best of both worlds: intimate and sociable areas.**

right **A mezzanine bedroom is both separate from, and yet part of, a double-height city pad.**

below **The tiniest of home offices, squeezed at one end of a room, provides the perfect retreat.**

space specifics

The best homes have a balance of great spaces. Be they boxy and modern, or a mix of big and small, it's not dimensions that matter, but the ebb and flow from intimate space to open-plan, and back again. Fit rooms together as snugly as jigsaw pieces, and your harmonious home is assured.

We all have individual space preferences. And by the time we become homeowners, our architectural tastes will be shaped not just by personality and lifestyle, but early influences and contemporary designs. The constraints of our property and budget, or the chance to move, also come into the equation.

how do you want your space?

Take time to crystallize your aspirations for the perfect space – now. Tune into your tastes. Do you focus on the charm of cottage-style rooms, or long for the open spaces offered by a warehouse conversion? Do you like the idea of a room for every activity, or the flexibility that interconnecting spaces brings? Look back to your lifestyle notes. Does the way you live life at home dovetail with your ideal space configuration?

above and right **Open-plan living isn't just a question of knocking down walls; it's a lifestyle choice. Would it suit you? Consider your personality, physical size, whether you are active or passive at home. Individuals who like to be snug and enveloped by a room may prefer the cosiness of four walls and a shut door, rather than acres of space.**

Consider finance. Decorating big rooms can be expensive. Think not just of huge windows to curtain or the extra square metreage of flooring, but the need to buy extra (or extra-large) furniture to fill the space. Heating and lighting requirements may also be more costly in open-plan areas.

Is privacy and noise control an issue, for you or members of your family? If peace is vital, then small rooms are preferable to zoned living. An interconnecting room makes a good alternative, if it's fitted with sound double doors. Or adapt the principle of the en suite bathroom. A tiny room within a room – created by stealing part of a sitting room, say – can form a particularly quiet zone.

Consider the bigger picture; not just individual room size, but how each space links and flows together.

Also consider the bigger picture; not just room size, but how each space links and flows together. Build in an element of surprise. Think of the drama of moving from a tiny hall to a big drawing room, or the almost secretive appeal of interlinked master bedroom, en suite bath, and dressing room, however small. Sometimes, carving out bespoke extra rooms makes the whole home more dynamic.

If there's the chance to alter the existing home template, but the property isn't as big as you

opposite **Decide whether you want home to be a retreat or an energizing space. For some, the low ceilings and small proportions of cottagey properties provide comfort; others find them unpleasantly restrictive.**

above **Don't underestimate the potential of a tiny hall. Fit it with double doors, and the transition from shady space to light-filled drawing room will be a constant pleasure.**

would like, then remember there are tricks to employ. If you need space to spread out, psychologically it's far better to create one large room where everyone can breathe (plus several little ones), than stick with two mediocre-sized rooms. Vertical volume, such as a double-height hall, can be as dramatic as one sprawling lateral space. And, properly planned, a cohesive link between ground floor and garden can visually (and physically) double your living space.

Everyone loves the freedom of a big room. There's space to spread out and socialize, plus the potential to change furniture arrangements. If your home doesn't have generous proportions, cost up alterations to create a large space that suits your needs.

big rooms

You will already know, from lifestyle planning, where – and why – a large room is most useful to you, be that a capacious family kitchen, or a luxurious master bedroom. Yet, whether dealing with existing or newly formed proportions, early on consciously evaluate its good and bad points. For all its potential, a wide, open space can be daunting: furniture may seem too small, wall expanses look alarmingly empty, or ambience be sadly lacking.

opposite **A large bedroom runs the risk of feeling like an impersonal hotel bedroom. To add atmosphere, create a seating zone in the spare space at the end of the bed. These armchairs are perfectly placed in front of a built-in TV.**

right **Use furniture scale to balance tall ceilings: this low, but very long, window bench looks nicely in proportion.**

Check out the proportions, and architectural features, in the room. Do they hang together comfortably? Are windows sufficiently lofty and doors tall enough to balance a vast floor area? In a moderate-sized room, the relatively simple device of replacing doors with floor-to-ceiling-height versions, or installing French doors instead of a sash window, can work wonders. Does the ceiling look suspiciously low? There may be a false ceiling. If there's a fireplace, it's vital that it is imposing enough to cope with generous dimensions; if not, then consider replacing it.

When you're confident the shell is in good shape, decide now on the key focal point. Every room needs one, but a visual anchor becomes more crucial in a large room. Perhaps the focus will be imposing double doors or aged timber beams? If there isn't an obvious feature, then decorative or furniture choices must dictate one. A chimney breast may be panelled with a subtle wood veneer, or an uninterrupted expanse of wall may call for a floor-to-ceiling mirror, or a good piece of art.

For some, a major plus of large rooms is the chance to luxuriate in 'spare' space, and enjoy the drama of scaled-up furniture. This is not the most cost-effective option, as you may need to find an extra-large sofa, or commission a custom-made dining table, simply to balance the space. On the other hand, you will require fewer key pieces. Don't spoil the elegantly sparse mood by filling available alcoves with built-in cupboards and shelves. It's far better to place a large free-standing cabinet or bookshelf centre stage on one wall.

this page **This generously proportioned drawing room is zoned into three areas. There's a window dining table for casual suppers, a capacious sofa for relaxing, and fireside chairs for conversation. If there's minimal floor area between each zone, then beef up 'visual' space by using spindly legged furniture and glass or Perspex tables, rather than solid pieces.**

opposite **Scaled-up sofas and tables are a must for filling up large rooms. In this modern space, modular contemporary seating is an ideal solution. Its L-shaped and daybed components can provide intimate corners for evening relaxing, but be pushed back against the walls for maximum floor space at parties.**

For others, the draw of a big room is precisely because a large space can accommodate lots of furniture. In a sitting room, say, several seating areas can be zoned around sofas at one end, with a chair and table at the other. The big room instantly becomes multi-functional, as well as having the potential to change its layout. If the purpose of having a large space is to cater for parties, though, formulate contingency plans for clearing the floor. There should be some furniture that is easily stacked, or light enough to be quickly rearranged into a more sociable configuration.

opposite **Despite its imposing pitched roof, this sitting room feels welcoming. The secret has been to paint the chimney breast alcoves in a muted colour, to reduce the apparent height of the ceiling. Symmetrical accessories, and the low-hung painting, also bring the eye level down.**

above left **A similar trick is employed in an attic bedroom. Deep colour is taken to only midway up the wall, so all attention is focused on the custom-built, low platform bed.**

above right **A high, pitched skylight can leave unfriendly expanses of white wall. Here, the space is used to dramatic advantage for a hanging.**

When you're confident the shell is in good shape, decide now on the key focal point. Every room needs one.

If a large room has a tall, vaulted or double-height ceiling, it can lack cosiness, and sound can echo unpleasantly. So you will need to employ visual tricks to bring the ceiling down. For example, if walls are painted, stop the colour at natural cornice height, instead of taking it right up to the ceiling. In a double-height space, pick one colour for the wall that bisects both levels, so that it becomes a decorative 'floating' feature in itself, distracting attention from a chimney-like void.

Decorative accessories are also good tools. A giant canvas (real art, or one painted by you) fills an empty vertical space more effectively than a number of little pictures. And a funky chandelier, hanging low, also distracts attention from an overpowering ceiling height. Think, too, about the dimensions of furniture. Even if cupboards or shelves are built-in, resist the temptation to take them right to the top, so they don't accentuate an already tall room. On the other hand, pieces mustn't be so low that they seem ridiculously small scale.

Often the most pressing reason for a giant space is that it creates a sociable kitchen, where eating, cooking and entertaining can coexist. Yet, having formed the space, it's a mistake to line both walls with cupboards, thus creating an unfriendly corridor effect. Far more attractive, not to mention user-friendly, is to plan the kitchen/eating zone with a central island, around which everyone can circulate. Design the island to include a breakfast bar for perching, plus useful storage. Visually, it'll look good as it breaks up the space. Practically, it will be one of the most popular areas in the room.

BIG ROOM CHECKLIST

- Decide why you want a big room. Is it to cater for a large family, or to create drama?
- List the room's good and bad architectural points. How can you correct/enhance them?
- What will the focal point be? Do you need to add one?
- What functions must the large space fulfil? How will you arrange furniture to create different activity zones?
- Will your furniture look in proportion? Do you need new?

below left **In a particularly spacious kitchen, an island can be scaled up to incorporate a sink and an extension breakfast bar, leaving walls free to carry streamlined units and large appliances.**

below right **An island unit makes a big kitchen look more intimate, doubles the available work surface, and becomes a key congregation spot.**

Often the reason for a giant space is that it creates a sociable kitchen, where eating, cooking and entertaining can coexist.

this *page* **Despite its cavernous double-height ceiling, this kitchen still feels inviting. The dining table takes the place of an island, nicely filling the space and yet straddling two distinct cooking and living zones. Spindly, rather than solid, chairs maintain a light, spacious mood.**

this page **The key to using large-scale pieces of furniture effectively in small spaces is to place them centrally, so circulation is easy. A multi-functional piece, like a sofa with built-in tables, or dining table with attached bench seating, creates a neater silhouette.**

There's no question that small rooms need maximum planning. Yet who can deny the cosy pleasures of a neatly proportioned bedroom, or the sociability of a dining room with enclosing walls?

small rooms

In today's scramble for open-plan, don't forget the appeal of the small room. They have a part to play in every home. In a modern warehouse, small rooms give welcome visual relief from wide-open spaces, promoting privacy and peace. In family houses, a string of them will accommodate extra bedrooms. And in space-compromised city pads or country cottages, small spaces are the norm from which we must squeeze maximum living quarters.

So appraise the small rooms you have, and check their dimensions. Architecturally speaking, little spaces are rarely

above **What this bedroom lacks in square metres, it makes up for in sophistication. If a small room lacks architectural detailing, panelled walls or a good selection of art provide an excellent visual distraction. Don't skimp on comfort. The multi-layered bed and cosy armchair make the room look much grander than the reality of its actual dimensions.**

left **Dark walls can streamline a tiny room, if furniture and accessories are kept to a minimum.**

accorded as much respect (and attention) as entertaining rooms, so skirting boards may be meanly proportioned, windows uninspiring, or fitted cupboards jammed in. Remedy these problems first, if necessary removing bad joinery, or even the door, if privacy isn't crucial. Draw up a to-scale floor plan, which you will need when planning what (and how much) furniture will fit.

right **Make full use of alcoves for squeezing in a bath or shower, so the space looks streamlined. An all-white scheme, from tiles to sanitary ware, always makes a tiny bathroom look bigger.**

opposite **Despite its low ceiling and modest scale, this sitting room feels sociable. The secret lies in picking comfortable, chunky, yet low furniture and accessories on a robust scale. Lamps, rather than overhead lighting, detract attention away from the beams.**

In city pads or country cottages, small spaces are the norm from which we must squeeze maximum living quarters.

above and below left **Just because a bathroom is tiny doesn't mean you must abandon chunky fittings full of character. Many roll-top baths (antique or new) come in smaller than average lengths, so can be particularly useful in small-scale en suite bathrooms or kids' washrooms. Look, too, for neatly proportioned pedestals or basins with an integral towel rail below. If there's no room elsewhere for a shower, then include one over the bath. Wall-mounted taps and minimal accessories keep the look simple.**

Compare the existing (or planned) room function for each small space, and see whether you've picked the best use for it. Do so in the context of the whole home, reviewing all rooms at once. It's tempting to assume little rooms are best reserved for bedrooms or home offices. But think twice. Instead of two children each occupying a small bedroom, wouldn't bunk beds free one, so it can become a laundry room? Isn't it better to install a study corner in the main living space, and turn a teeny ground-floor study into a walk-in cloakroom, relieving pressure on a narrow hall? Sometimes, by swapping functions, a small room struggling to fulfil its potential rises to a new challenge.

left **There's a real appeal to an eaves bedroom, despite its inevitable small proportions and compromised ceiling height. Maximize intimacy by making the bed a focal point, layering on cosy textiles and pillows, but keep patterns subdued, otherwise they will fight with ceiling beams. Built-in furniture can be problematic beneath a pitched roof. While most clothes and books can be stored in chests or shelves, long hanging space may need to go in a landing cupboard.**

above right **It's fairly easy to squeeze a bathroom beneath the eaves, but harder to install a proper shower enclosure, if ceiling heights are low. If beams are old, and very prominent, stick to a simple, no-nonsense style.**

above **If converting the attic into new bedrooms, it's worth pricing a bathroom as well. Guests or children won't want to climb down an extra flight of stairs to wash, and a bath, basin and loo can be squeezed into a really minute space.**

opposite **Despite potentially small proportions, an attic room frequently feels bigger because of good light – often from a Velux window – and a high ceiling. Play these up with a high bedhead and light-diffusing window treatments.**

It's a common misconception that large furniture clutters up a small room. In fact, the reverse is true.

Don't despair of a minute kitchen or bathroom, as these are the easiest small rooms to plan. In kitchens, make the most of slim appliances and wall-mounted cupboards, arranging units in a galley or L-shape to aid traffic flow. If the room is tiny, with a high ceiling, avoid very tall wall cupboards and replace with open shelves. Review what goes into the kitchen. Could the washing machine, say, go in a shower room, or the garage?

In a bathroom, double-check if the people who use it prefer baths or showers. A shower takes up less room than a bath, and can be incorporated into a streamlined wet room. If a bath is preferred, butting it against one wall isn't necessarily space-saving. A smaller than average roll-top, centrally placed, promotes traffic flow and makes the room seem larger. Wall-mounted sanitary ware will also maximize the floor space.

above **If a kitchen is small but tall-ceilinged, high wall-mounted cupboards provide valuable storage. This minute space is so well planned there's even room for a banquette, with built-in storage.**

centre **Balance useful slimline appliances with robust pieces that make a kitchen look bigger.**

far right **Plan to streamline large appliances. Neatly sunk into a false partition wall, this capacious fridge all but disappears in a small galley.**

Although charming, low cottage ceilings can play havoc with proportions. So consider visual tricks to prevent claustrophobia. Check that a fire surround isn't too large for the room, replace a dangling pendant light with ceiling-mounted spots, and plan treatments that elongate, rather than foreshorten, windows: full-length curtains, not tiny blinds. Low-slung pieces – slouchy sofas to slim benches – keep the furniture line (and eye level) down.

It's a common misconception that large furniture clutters up a small room. In fact, the reverse is true. So use scale cleverly, to trick the eye. A four-poster bed can make a bedroom ceiling seem higher; a generous round table sociably fills a dining room. The key is to keep furniture shapes streamlined, accessories bold

yet minimal, and – most importantly – plan room layouts for ease of movement. Juggle the floor plan, using cutouts of furniture, to find the best arrangement.

Choice of decoration goes a long way towards creating a harmonious space. Given that many little rooms lack grand windows, go with the flow and play up moody natural lighting with dark colours. Trying to compensate for low lighting by painting rooms in white, or pastel shades, simply doesn't work. Avoid clichéd small-room colours, like dark red or green, and pick subtle, muted shades like greys or taupes, more tranquil and good-looking in natural and artificial light. Plain surfaces are best, either paint, panelling or wood veneers. A room will seem bigger if the borders between individual planes (walls, floors, ceiling) are blurred. So try painting everything in one colour, or take a timber or leather covered floor up the walls as well.

In today's multi-tasking world, open-plan living – where people can cook, relax and work simultaneously – is popular. Spawned by city warehouse living, it's now a concept just as likely to be used in a traditional home. But remember that this is a lifestyle choice, as well as a decorative one. Communicative and sociable it may be, but peace and privacy become harder to find.

open-plan areas and zoning

A typical open-plan space combines kitchen, dining and sitting areas, with no physical division in between. Less commonly, mezzanine-level sleeping platforms may be dropped into the space or, most radically, an open-plan bedroom and bath sprawl across one complete level. More modest variations might include an open-plan ground floor, with bedrooms upstairs, or a zoned kitchen/dining/relaxing space, with a separate formal sitting room.

You will already know from lifestyle planning if open-plan life appeals, and if – financially – it's an option. Most buildings have

opposite **In this cleverly designed conversion, a mezzanine study has been neatly dropped into the double height of the chief living space. Lined with books, it has a quiet ambience, yet is visually all of a piece with the main area.**

above right **Double-height spaces cry out for a good collection of wall art.**

right **Some staircases become the main feature of an open-plan space. Others, as here, are discreetly hidden behind a partition wall.**

the potential to be transformed. But the work can be radical, expensive, and long-term. You will need a good builder and probably an architect, not to mention a structural engineer, who will guide you through the minefield of what can (and can't) be removed. So think carefully. Just making one room open-plan involves complex planning.

If you want free rein, consider buying a loft-style apartment or converted warehouse. The latter are usually shells, with just a water and electrical supply. On the plus side is the freedom of choosing where everything goes. On the money side, you'll need an architect and/or builder to do the work.

When an entire ground floor becomes open-plan, it's not enough to create a single big space. Where will storage go? How will you conceal essential services? What about access to upstairs: will there be a design-statement staircase, dramatically bisecting the space, or will it be discreetly screened? If you've opted for one-level living, how will you create private bed- and bathrooms?

One good solution is a Tardis-style enclosed structure, which can include everything from the washing machine and a guest loo, to storage. It's also a convenient location to site radiators. Placed centrally, it becomes an informal division between spaces, too. Alternatively, devise a 'pod', which may be designed to bisect right through two floors. In here, all the 'wet' rooms can be contained, from laundry room to loo and showers, so that plumbing is restricted to (and concealed within) one area.

Unless there are small rooms off the main space, the open-plan environment must allow for quiet areas and bedrooms, too.

opposite **A central structure, comprising cloakroom and storage, divides – yet unifies – an open-plan living floor in a city house. While wall colours and floor are the same throughout, each zone has an individual, anchoring feature. In the sitting room, a rug softens the space. In the dining room, there's an elaborate chandelier. And the route past cloakroom to kitchen is expertly lit with pendant lights.**

this page **An open-plan kitchen/dining room can be as useful as an entire floor devoted to one-space living. Here the key divider – the island unit – has storage on the kitchen side and a breakfast bar on the other.**

For these, sliding floor-to-ceiling doors, or partition walls with a conventional door, are essential. It's a good idea to divide the open-plan area according to peaceful, and activity, zones. Or consider a mezzanine platform (for study or sleep), which allows you to communicate with people below, yet experience a sense of separation.

Even in a small open-plan space, it's vital to have some physical divisions. These may already be in place, such as load-bearing sections of wall. Turn these to advantage by lining them with bookshelves or building in cupboards. Floor-to-ceiling MDF or sandblasted glass sliding doors can also help section off a kitchen from a sitting space, for example. For a less conventional take on dividing structures, consider a section of curved

Placing the table between the kitchen and the sitting areas marks out the logical progression from cooking to chilling out.

wall, which may hide a kitchen from relaxation zones. Also consider free-standing furniture, which may be moved around to suit.

Divisions needn't all be vertical. Think, too, of horizontal methods for dividing up an open-plan space. Double-height areas, for example, can lack intimacy, so consider installing a deliberately low, false ceiling over certain zones, perhaps the dining

area. This can also be a useful device for concealing pipes and wires. If there's a mezzanine platform already in place, think about the most suitable activity zone to site below it. Think, too, of creating 'stepped' floor levels, so that one walks down into a relaxing zone, or up steps to a sleeping platform.

Firm up structural decisions in conjunction with your lifestyle plans, so you really do get activity zones in the right place. Even if there's an architect on the job, they will appreciate your input. So draw up rough floor plans, marked with windows, doors, and so on, and sketch ideas. Most good architects will come up with three, often very different, variations on a theme. The more you communicate with them, the more tailor-made their plans can be.

Once the basic structure is assured, it's time to formally 'zone' spaces. However much you enjoy an impromptu environment, it's vital to know where sofas will go, or where you plan to eat,

all pictures **Not all open-plan spaces are conveniently square. Yet, despite being long and thin, the shape of this living area has been turned to its advantage. By placing the kitchen at one end, dining room in the centre and sitting room at the other end, living zones are well defined. The furniture, with its dark woods, suedes and cream linens, has been picked with a careful eye, so there's a consistent vision from every corner of the space. A tall mirror, placed in the sitting zone, neatly bounces views from one end to the other.**

so that lighting and power points can be installed accordingly. Furniture arrangement plays a big part in zoning, but so too do decoration, flooring, colour and ambience. First, return to the notes on human traffic flow. What will be the most commonly trodden routes through the space? In an open-plan area, it's inevitable that certain sections will turn into corridors. Plan for that, and arrange furniture accordingly.

Eating areas should be close to the kitchen, so food arrives at the table hot, and dishwasher loading is easy. It's a good idea to plan two zones. First, an informal breakfast bar, either built-in to the kitchen, or at a separate island unit. Add stools or benches, which can easily be transported for use in another area (at a desk, say, or a child's bedroom). There should also be a formal dining table, which can double as a work station for a computer. Placing the table between the kitchen and the sitting areas is

upholstered seating in an open-plan space, you must be able to move it around easily. So add castors, and ensure that the floor is robust enough to cope with frequent movement.

Zone lighting, too. In a busy kitchen area, you'll want good overhead illumination, probably from low-voltage ceiling lights, plus work-surface task lighting. Over the dining table, an adjustable pendant light will be more appropriate, and, in the sitting area, restrict illumination to table lamps or floor-standing lights to promote atmosphere. Try to have the kitchen lights on a different circuit to those in the dining room and sitting room, so that

often the best location. It marks out the logical progression from cooking to chilling out.

Pick upholstered seating that allows for a choice of configurations. Two identical sofas are useful, as they may be placed opposite one another for an intimate mood, or back to back, one pointing towards the TV, the other towards the kitchen, if different people want to pursue varied activities. Add some armchairs, and sociable U-shapes or L-shapes are also possible. Modern, modular seating, which may include daybeds, sofas, and stools, is also a good choice. To get the best out of

this page **A design-statement staircase can be used at once to divide, and to unify, an open-plan area. It's a dramatic device, because it creates tantalizing glimpses from one space to another. Look for staircase designs that won't impede light flow, or block views. Open or glass treads, glass panel or vertical metal balusters, or a light-refracting glass landing are all good options.**

left **In an open-plan space with double-height ceilings, a full-height partition wall may look out of proportion. This one creates a division, yet still allows light to permeate the space.**

below **Not all bathrooms need to be fully closed off. Here, a slim partition wall is all that's required.**

decorated with a strong and simple vision. At its most basic, this means one floor throughout, and a few key hard surfaces, to be repeated in varying quantities around the space.

Yet just as, within a conventional house, there's the need for the contrast between large and small rooms, light and dark tones, upbeat and moody ambience, it's vital to engineer a similar mix within

Furniture arrangement plays a big part in zoning an open-plan space, but so too do decoration, flooring, colour and ambience.

glaring overhead illumination can be switched off for relaxing. Fit dimmer switches wherever possible. Also remember to install central floor plugs, so that table lamps in a central seating zone can be plugged in without trailing wires.

When it comes to planning colours and surfaces, remember that open-plan spaces afford constant glimpses and vistas from one area to another. You are also very likely to move furniture around. So, for the space to feel cohesive, it must be

above left, centre and right
One of the chief pleasures of open-plan living is to be able to cook and socialize at the same time. Yet not everyone wants the kitchen on show, especially the dirty dishes. In this city apartment, the kitchen is cleverly contained within a box-style construction. Day to day, the door is left open to improve light and human traffic flow. During entertaining, it can be firmly shut. On the other side of the kitchen wall, the 'box' has been designed to incorporate cloakroom storage.

left **Every open-plan space needs a quiet area for study, be that on a mezzanine platform or on a galleried landing.**

Remember that open-plan spaces afford constant glimpses and vistas from one area to another.

an open-plan space. Floors can be individualized. On timber boards, rugs may brighten or delineate areas. Tiled or concrete floors may be decorated with sections of inset contrast colour, or a lino floor spiced up with motifs. Colourwise, it makes sense to stick to the one-palette guideline. Use key tones to distinguish wall sections, or to colour-code tranquil, active or play zones. And a good tonal mix will help carve out moody areas, and bright, upbeat areas, from one similarly lit space.

left and above **In this one-level family apartment, the kitchen has been sociably planned to lie at the heart of the flat, opposite the front door, and immediately adjacent to the formal sitting room. Cleverly, it has sliding doors on two sides, so that guests don't need to look at the after-dinner chaos, and small children can be kept out of the way of appliances.**

OPEN-PLAN CHECKLIST

● Why do you want an open-plan space? Improved communication, to make a design statement?

● Is finance available for turning a ground floor into an open-plan zone? Or should you buy a shell?

● Will you employ an architect? Or a builder and structural engineer to work to your own design?

● What key zones do you require? Plan for places to cook, relax, eat, socialize and work.

● Will your existing furniture suit a new, big space?

opposite **When rooms face one another, parallel arches instead of doors allow the spaces to be linked, yet separate. These rooms play with tonal contrasts, switching from moody sitting-room walls, to a dark corridor floor, to a white room beyond.**

left **One or two carefully chosen accessories can transform 'dead' landing space into a pretty vista.**

right **In a narrow hall, it's vital to create a light-filled view through to the garden beyond.**

Whatever size our property is, we all have a front door and hall, corridors or landings, and frequently stairs. Yet these traffic areas are often the Cinderella spaces at home, overlooked in the rush to plan rooms. So reverse that trend, and create practical surfaces, good lighting and inspiring decoration, not to mention enticing vistas to be glimpsed and enjoyed on the way from room to room.

traffic areas and linking vistas

It's vital to set the right visual and practical note in the entrance hall. For you, it must be a user-friendly point where coats can be deposited, family greeted and everyday cares left behind. For visitors, it must feel welcoming.

Start by surveying what you have. Are the hall/landing/stairs dark, or is there a pleasant view to the garden? Is it easy to move through to a reception room, or is the corridor narrow? If building work is possible, get the configuration right now. Replacing an ordinary door with an archway or double doors (check fire regulations) can aid traffic flow. A skylight above a stairwell will flood sunshine in; in a corridor, replacing wood door panels with glass will improve light flow.

Visually, traffic areas should be planned in conjunction with the whole home palette. But decide now whether these spaces should blend seamlessly into

tight, a wall-mounted console shelf is a good bet. Is heating sufficient in the hall, for a warm welcome?

Pay particular attention to lighting. In a typical house, you're aiming for good illumination in the hall, so it's not gloomy, but add a dimmer switch, so you can crank up the ambience when entertaining. Corridors should be lit with low-voltage wall lamps, at regular intervals. If you have a feature staircase, then stair-level lights can make a dramatic feature. And do plan lighting circuits so that you can turn off the hall light while ascending the stairs to bed, and vice versa.

Then concentrate on those vistas. If you've planned a careful colour palette, visual links will be assured. But travel around the house, and see which views can be enhanced. If there's a stretch of bare wall, place a pretty chair to be glimpsed from the corridor, or dress a landing window with unlined curtains, to add character to the space.

rooms, or provide contrast. For a linked look, you might choose timber for the ground floor, running uninterrupted from hall to kitchen, as well as up stair treads. Polished plaster walls might repeat from landings to reception rooms. By contrast, you might plan moody colours for hall and corridors, and a pale scheme for rooms, providing a refreshing jolt on moving from staircase to living zones.

Traffic areas must function practically. It's useful, and attractive, to include furniture in the hall, but check that pieces are slim enough for people to pass by, and that accessories won't knock over. If space is

above left **Adding a 'window' section in a wall promotes light flow, and gives intriguing views from room to room. Glass-panelled doors create a similar effect.**

left **Avoid a dark corridor in a city flat by having a room with natural light at each end. Here, the view stretches from end to end.**

opposite **It's a common error to impede visual flow from landing to bedrooms by abrupt changes in colour or flooring. These rooms feel harmoniously linked.**

In traditional properties, interconnecting rooms are a sympathetic answer to open-plan living. Two rooms are linked by a central aperture (arched or square), which may be fitted with double or sliding doors. There's the advantage of sociable living, and the chance for privacy. Some period homes were designed with connected rooms for 'withdrawing' after dinner, or around a flowing *enfilade* of rooms. In less grand, or less old, homes, knock through a dividing wall to make an interconnected room.

interconnecting rooms

this page **A knocked-through drawing room will be more cohesive if there's a centrally placed piece of furniture, rather than an empty space. A long, low stool is a good choice: it doesn't impede the view between rooms, and can be drawn into either area.**

opposite **If there are pendant lights in each room, ensure they match, or are similarly themed. If only one room has a decent cornice, consider getting it copied for the other.**

In many homes, the adaptability of an interconnected room is a boon. For a start, fitted with double doors, it offers the potential to create a communicative open space, or two separate rooms. The former guarantees a good family area and party room, and the latter, instant privacy, quiet, and intimacy for quieter social gatherings. The configuration works well for varied needs. It's the most sensible link between kitchen and dining room, and can create a multi-functional sitting room, allowing for separate TV-watching and relaxing areas. More luxurious still is the option of master bedroom, interconnected bathroom, and even dressing room.

Whether you've inherited an interconnected room, or want to create one, review good and bad points. In narrow houses, the device provides the one chance for a room to capture valuable sunlight, front and back. Room proportions are unaffected, because you're not removing an entire wall, just

this page **In an elegant, formal home, it's a better idea to keep the dining table in the kitchen, and use double doors to create a link between drawing room and kitchen. This way, clutter isn't on view, and cooking smells can be contained. When planning surfaces and a colour scheme, linking materials must be practical enough for kitchen use, yet sophisticated enough to take their place in a drawing room. Here, timber flooring is ideal for both.**

opposite **In this simple, family living space, the double doors remain hooked neatly back against the walls day to day. Yet, for formal dinner parties, there's the option to shut off the kitchen. By including a table in each space, kids can eat in one room, and grown-ups in the other.**

a central linking section. In a knocked-through period drawing room, for example, both fireplaces remain, leaving a focus for each space. And original features, such as cornice work, stay in place.

Think through potential disadvantages. Will noise control be difficult? Might cooking smells waft into the sitting area? If the only bathroom is linked to your bedroom, is that tricky for guests? There are practicalities, too. For example, original timber boards will need to be relaid to make the new gap look seamless.

Do get appropriate design/building advice and planning consent, as the removal of a load-bearing wall will require a supporting beam. If rooms have high ceilings, the aperture must be appropriately lofty; too low, and you will spoil the drama of the room. The new gap will need to be replastered and the room redecorated. If double or sliding doors are to be fitted, what are the logistics of where they sit when open? Can they fold back flat on either side of the gap? If not, will people bang into them?

Whether you've inherited an interconnected room, or want to create one, review good and bad points. In narrow houses, it's the one chance for a room to capture valuable sunlight, front and back.

Decoratively speaking, it's crucial for interconnecting rooms to hang together. Lay an identical floor throughout, keep window treatments the same, and plan a harmonious colour scheme. Furniture should be subtly themed, rather than slavishly matched. Within the cohesive framework, use lighting and accessories to play with mood. An interconnected space should work as a whole, but – when the doors are shut – each area should have an individual character, and ambience, of its own.

opposite and left **Consider whether a view from outside to inside works well. Create as many visual links as possible. In this space, the designers have picked a subtle grey-green for the paint colour above and below the printed wall hanging, to tone prettily with the foliage-only city garden. Likewise, the purple-brown leather chairs pick out the metal-toned panels, immediately above the sliding glass doors.**

below **In a family house, where bikes or toys are likely, plan for ways to conceal them in the back yard. Here, the dark tones of bamboo fencing blend nicely with the rich walnut within, and behind it is a space for all the family's paraphernalia.**

outdoor connections

However beautiful an interior, our eyes are naturally drawn towards the space outside. Plan for that. Review what's on offer outdoors, smarten it up, and ensure there's a smooth transition from inside to out.

With today's increasingly relaxed lifestyles, it's more common than ever to merge indoor–outdoor boundaries. Climate pays its part. In cooler climes, seeing the great outdoors must be as much part of the plan as physically joining the two together. Look first at exit points, whether that's to a garden or

city yard. Are they usefully positioned in a key living area, so outdoors is immediately accessible? If not, can a back door be moved, a window replaced with a glass-panelled door, or new French doors set into a garden-facing sitting room?

There's more potential if building work, or a new extension, is planned. Many contemporary ground-floor extensions feature floor-to-ceiling sliding or fold-back glass doors creating a 'wall' of glass overlooking outdoors. It's a substantial investment, but your available living space is doubled, provided weather is good. Indoors, there's extra sunshine. And there's that great view beyond. If a bedroom or bathroom leads directly onto a roof terrace or balcony, consider installing French doors here, too.

Referring back to your lifestyle notes, consider the best location for a connection. If entertaining is common, site the new doors to link dining room and patio. For families, access

Remember that floor-to-ceiling glass or French doors will frame the view onto the great outdoors. So it must stay neat and tidy at all times.

should be directly off the kitchen, rather than a formal drawing room; otherwise, smart furnishings may get ruined. How you use the new link will directly affect the features and furniture which go outside. If summer eating is popular, then a kitchen/deck arrangement is ideal, with outdoors table and chairs.

Remember that floor-to-ceiling glass or French doors will frame the view onto the great outdoors. So it must stay neat and tidy at all times. Plan plants that look good even in winter (a garden

above left **The beauty of planning outdoors and indoors in tandem means that great outdoor features, like a stunning view, can be taken into account. In this bedroom, the greenery outside prompted a simple all-white scheme, so that the eye travels straight out to enjoy the view.**

centre and above **A covered porch means you can decorate an indoor room and outdoor space to match, so the in–out mix is seamless. Here, Philippe Starck furniture and lighting, and gloss-painted white boards, are chic, yet practical: chairs may be carried in or out to suit.**

above and left **In summer, when eating outside may be a daily event, it makes sense to relocate the dining table outdoors, and take quick meals at the breakfast bar. So when planning a deck, ensure it's big enough to take a table, with room for lounger chairs as well. Plan flooring that blends with indoors, as well as the character of the house. Here, white boards echo its white-painted shingled exterior.**

centre will advise), and in a small yard, ensure that the back wall is prettily concealed with a creeper, or an attractive fence. Dovetail indoor/outdoor furniture styles: if the kitchen is modern, then choose trendy outdoor chairs to match. Identical flooring, running from inside to out, reinforces a seamless link. Hard-wearing, smart choices include concrete, limestone and solid timber decking.

With its white shingling, dark roof and luxuriant vegetation, the exterior of this modest house provides inspiration for a tranquil and homogeneous interior. Inside, contrasts of white paint and glossy wood enhance sunshine and shadows, and glass, white ceramics and greenery create decorative links from room to room.

space specifics case study

opposite **In a house comfortably linked with its surroundings, you need adaptable furniture. These chairs look as at home on the back porch as at the kitchen table.**

this page **The symmetrical look of the house is repeated in the carefully linked rooms. From the central hall, a visitor can form a complete circle, turning right into the drawing room, through the dining room, left into a second sitting room, alighting back in the hall. There's also access front to back through the hall to the kitchen and garden.**

Here is a house at one with, and inspired by, its setting. Surrounded by garden, with windows on all sides, there are views of greenery from every room. And precisely because of the trees, the interior is dark and shady. The owner has chosen to harness these powerful natural starting points, and forged a decorative scheme accordingly. There are only two surface choices: bright white paint, and rich, dark timber. Used upstairs and down, they shape a cohesive, harmonious interior.

Liberally used on all walls, trim woodwork, and floors upstairs, the fresh white paint serves two purposes. For one, it reduces walls and windows to a blank canvas, enhancing the crispness of the views of vegetation beyond. Secondly, it captures what sunlight there is, and enhances the flow of light. By contrast, dark floorboards work with the inevitable gloom and create a moody ambience.

This light/dark theme creates extra visual pace as one travels through the house. At ground level, flooring throughout is in the grown-up solid dark timber boards, in keeping with the entertaining areas. The stair treads are also in dark wood. Yet the second the visitor alights at the first floor bedroom and bathroom suite, the floorboards are painted in bright, white gloss. The look is fresher, and the mood consequently more relaxed.

Cleverly, all furniture except upholstered pieces plays up the negative–positive contrasts. There's the dark-wood bateau lit and a heavy bookcase in the main sitting room, and more relaxed pieces such as white-painted tables and chairs. The furniture mixes and matches varying degrees of light and shade. In the casual kitchen, all pieces are white. In the sitting room, most are dark. And in the dining room, which links the two together, the table is white and the chairs dark wood.

Precisely because the palette is neutrals-only, there's more opportunity to play with textures. There's a deliberate mix at work here. Ceilings are

above left **By painting furniture, as well as walls, white, the owner throws attention onto the green vegetation through the windows, which are sensibly free from fussy curtains or blinds.**

above right **Even cupboard interiors are tied into the light–dark theme.**

far left **In a home where rooms are all interlinked, and there are constant vistas from one doorway to another, it's even more vital that a decorative scheme is cohesive.**

left **In the formal dining room, where a softer ambience is required, the owner has rung the changes by hanging an unlined linen blind in a soft curve across the window, teamed with a low-slung candelabra.**

this page, inset left
To improve light flow in a dark interior, and to create a physical link from dining room to drawing room, the door has been removed.

this page **In the drawing room, which is entered via a doorway just off the hall, and exited by a second, directly into the dining room, good furniture placement is key. By positioning two similar-sized sofas opposite one another, with a coffee table in between, there's plenty of room to circulate.**

this picture and left **Despite its modest proportions, this small room has still been filled with large-scale pieces, and consequently feels sophisticated and cosy. The daybed is cleverly placed at an angle, allowing easy access to the bed, yet making the most of** **an intimate under-eaves sloping roof.**

right **The space potential of a relatively small bathroom was maximized by building a partition wall to create a nook for the bath, then placing the loo out of sight, just behind.**

Cleverly, all furniture except upholstered pieces has been picked to play up the negative—positive contrasts.

gloss white and furniture is in highly polished wood, to reflect light. By contrast, there's dense, heavy linen for upholstery and window treatments. Even accessories fall neatly into the glossy/crunchy categories. Storm lanterns and white platters are prettily light-reflective, while cotton throws and coir mats repeat the homespun textile theme.

The discreet architectural detailing within is clearly inspired by the original exterior without. The white shingling repeats itself upstairs, in the

white-painted boards, and downstairs, with narrow tongue-and-groove in the dining room. The original panelled front door provides a template for built-in cupboards, plainly panelled to match. And, on the exterior porch, white decking echoes the shingling, stopping only as the house ends and green grass begins.

At the core of this tightly wrought, simple scheme is the evident plainness of all surfaces and materials. There are no patterned fabrics, household items are unadorned, and there are no pictures – just mirrors – on the walls. Yet, far from creating a boring interior, it's clear that this is a device to play up the prettiness outside. Once placed in a simple glass vase, cut roses or sprigs of foliage take on just as much beauty as the impact of the garden beyond.

source directory

PROFESSIONAL BODIES

British Interior Design Association

1/4 Chelsea Harbour Design
  Centre
Chelsea Harbour
London SW10 0XE
020 7349 0800

www.bida.org

Listings of professional interior designers, countrywide.

The Building Centre

26 Store Street
London WC1E 7BT
020 7692 4000

www.buildingcentre.co.uk

Useful information on many building products.

CORGI

0870 401 2300

www.corgi-group.com

Supplies information on CORGI registered fitters for installing new boilers/radiators/fires.

Heating and Hot Water Information Council

36 Holly Walk
Leamington Spa
Warwickshire CV32 4LY
0845 6002200

www.centralheating.co.uk

User-friendly website offering consumer information on central heating and hot water systems.

The Institution of Structural Engineers

11 Upper Belgrave Street
London SW1X 8BH
020 7235 4535

www.istructe.org.uk and
www.findanengineer.com

Lists the full membership of qualified structural engineers.

Royal Institute of British Architects Client Services

66 Portland Place
London W1B 1AD
020 7307 3700

www.architecture.com

Members' directory, plus advice on choosing an architect.

Royal Institute of Chartered Surveyors

12 Great George Street
Parliament Square
London SW1P 3AD
0870 3331600

www.rics.org.uk

List of members, plus advice on buying, selling and surveys.

WINDOWS/SLIDING DOORS

Crittall Windows

Springwood Drive
Braintree
Essex CM7 2YN
01376 324106

www.crittall-windows.co.uk

Authentic steel windows to suit 1930s- to 1950s-style homes.

DR Services (London)

Plumpton House
Plumpton Road
Hoddesdon, Herts EN11 0LB
01992 447122

www.drservices.co.uk

Made-to-measure sliding glass/metal/timber doors.

The Original Box Sash Window Company

The Joinery
29–30 The Arches
Alma Road, Windsor SL4 1QZ
01753 858196

www.boxsash.com

Authentic replicas of period-style windows.

Pellfold Parthos

1 The Quadrant
Howarth Road
Maidenhead
Berkshire SL6 1AP
01628 773353

www.designs4space.com

A selection of solid and glass partitions for large spaces.

Velux

Woodside Way
Glenrothes
Fife KY7 4ND
0870 3810740

www.velux.co.uk

Vast selection of roof windows.

RADIATORS/FIREPLACES

Bisque

244 Belsize Road
London NW6 4BT
020 7328 2225

www.bisque.co.uk

Huge range of contemporary radiators, from floor-level to panels, convectors to towel rails.

The Floor Warming Company

2 School Parade
High Street
Harefield UB9 6BT
01895 825288

www.floorwarmingcompany.co.uk

Suppliers and installers of electric underfloor heating systems.

LASSCO RBK

41 Maltby Street
London SE1 3PA
020 7394 2102

www.lassco.co.uk

Vast selection of reconditioned cast-iron radiators, including school styles.

Nu-Heat

Heathpark House
Devonshire Road
Heathpark Industrial Estate
Honiton, Devon EX14 1SD
01404 549770

www.nu-heat.co.uk

Suppliers of water-based underfloor heating sytems.

The Platonic Fireplace Company

Phoenix Wharf, Eel Pie Island
Twickenham TW1 3DY
020 8891 5904

www.platonicfireplaces.co.uk

Modern fireplaces and surrounds.

Real Flame

80 New Kings Road
London SW6 4LT
020 7731 2704

www.realflame.co.uk

Made-to-measure authentic period gas fires and surrounds.

LIGHTING DESIGNERS

John Cullen Lighting

585 Kings Road
London SW6 2EH
020 7371 5400

www.johncullenlighting.co.uk

Offers a design service and a wide range of discreet fittings.

Lighting Design International

Zero Ellelaine Road
London W6 9NZ
020 7381 8999

www.lightingdesigninternational.com

Lighting design for large residential projects.

SKK Lighting

34 Lexington Street
London W1F OLH
020 7434 4095

www.skk.net

Modern lighting specialists offering bespoke products and lighting consultancy.

AUDIO-VISUAL AND HOME MANAGEMENT SYSTEMS

Gibson Music

Unit 8, The Broomhouse
50 Sulivan Road
London SW6 3DX
020 7384 2270

www.gibson-music.com

Specialists in audio-visual and home management systems.

Musical Images

18 Monmouth Street
London WC2H 9HB
020 7497 1346

Specialist suppliers and installers of home-entertainment systems.

ARCHITECTURAL JOINERY/DETAILING

Aristocast

2 Wardsend Road
Sheffield S6 1RQ
0114 2690900

www.plasterware.net

Cornice and ceiling rose designs in fibrous plaster, own range as well as made-to-measure service.

Charles Codrington

Creative Wood
17 Trent Road
London SW2 5BJ
07930 406610

Streamlined bespoke cabinets in a choice of woods, or ready-to-paint MDF.

Charles Hurst Workshop

Unit 21
Bow Triangle Business Centre
Eleanor Street
London E3 4NP
020 8981 8562

Well-proportioned and simply styled architectural joinery.

Oakleaf Reproductions

Lingbob Mill, Main Street
Willesden, Bradford
West Yorkshire BD15 0JP
01535 272878

www.oakleaf.co.uk

Resin-based material Jacobean-style panelling, pre-stained or ready to paint.

DECORATIVE DETAILING

Forbes & Lomax

205a St John's Hill
London SW11 1TH
020 7738 0202

www.forbesandlomax.co.uk

Switches, sockets and dimmers in invisible perspex, frosted acrylic and metals.

Hafele

Swift Valley Industrial Estate
Rugby, Warwickshire CV21 1RD
01788 542020

www.hafele.co.uk

Architectural ironmongery and furniture fittings in every style.

Haute Deco

556 Kings Road
London SW6 2DZ
020 7736 7171

www.doorknobshop.com

Decorative resin and metal classic and modern doorknobs.

Knobs & Knockers

567 Kings Road
London SW6 2EB
020 7384 2884

www.knobs-and-knockers.com

Modern and period knobs, grilles and window fittings in polished brass, chrome and nickel.

Nu-Line

305–317 Westbourne Park Road
London W11 1EF
020 7727 7748

www.nu-line.net

Architectural ironmongery.

SURFACES

World's End Tiles

British Rail Yard
Silverthorne Road
London SW8 3HE
020 7819 2110

www.worldsendtiles.co.uk

Vast range of porcelain, natural stone, glass and ceramic tiles.

The Hardwood Flooring Company

146–152 West End Lane
London NW6 1SD
020 7328 8481

www.hardwoodflooring company.com

Big choice of new timber flooring, solid or engineered boards, in finishes including oak, beech, ash and maple.

Junckers

Wheaton Court Commercial Centre
Wheaton Road
Witham
Essex CM8 3UJ
01376 534700

www.junckers.com

Wide selection of solid hardwood floors and worktops.

Preedy Glass

Lamb Works
North Road
London N7 9DP
020 7700 0377

www.preedyglass.com

Made-to-order glass specialists, offering colour-back glass for worktops and surfaces, interior glass doors and glass floors.

Stone Age

Unit 3, Parsons Green Depot
Parsons Green Lane
London SW6 4HH
020 7384 9090

www.stone-age.co.uk

Over 80 limestone and sandstone choices, flooring and worktops made to order.

Stonell

Forstal House
Beltring
Paddock Wood
Kent TN12 6PY
01892 833500

www.stonell.com

Limestone, slate, marble floor tiles and granite worktops made to order.

COLOURS

Dulux Decorator Service

0845 7697668

www.duluxdecorator.co.uk

Useful paint advice and colour-matching service.

Farrow & Ball

249 Fulham Road
London SW3 6HY
020 7351 0273

www.farrow-ball.com

Range of 132 paint colours, available in all standard interior finishes, plus matching garden and exterior range. Co-ordinating wallpapers too.

Paint and Paper Library

5 Elystan Place
London SW3 3NT
020 7823 7755

www.paintlibrary.co.uk

Vast range of excellent paint colours, colour-matching service available.

Papers and Paints

4 Park Walk
London SW10 0AD
020 7352 8626

www.colourman.com

Huge range of paint colours including historical ranges. Colour-matching service available on request.

picture credits

The publishers would like to thank all those who allowed us to photograph their homes for this book.

All photography by Jan Baldwin **KEY**: **a** = above, **b** = below, **r** = right, **l** = left, **c** = centre.

Endpapers The owner of Tessuti, Catherine Vindevogel-Debal's house in Kortrijk, Belgium; **1** The family house EVLB in Bruges, Belgium, designed by architect Vincent Van Duysen; **2–3** A family home in Parsons Green, London. Architecture by Nicholas Helm and Yasuyuki Fukuda (architectural assistant) of Helm Architects. Interior design and all material finishes supplied by Maria Speake of Retrouvius Reclamation & Design; **4** The Fitzwilliam-Lay's family home. Architecture by Totem Design, interior design by Henri Fitzwilliam-Lay and Totem Design; **5** Interior decorator and designer for the firm Sibyl Colefax & John Fowler, Philip Hooper's own flat in London; **6** A family home in Parsons Green, London. Architecture by Nicholas Helm and Yasuyuki Fukuda (architectural assistant) of Helm Architects. Interior design and all material finishes supplied by Maria Speake of Retrouvius Reclamation & Design; **8** The Campbell family's apartment in London, architecture by Voon Wong Architects; **9r** Wendy Jansen and Chris Van Eldik, owners of J.O.B. Interieur's house in Wijk bij Duurstede, The Netherlands; **10–11** & **11a** Michael D'Souza of Mufti; **11b** Designer Tricia Foley's Long Island home; **12a** The owner of Tessuti, Catherine Vindevogel-Debal's house in Kortrijk, Belgium; **12b** The family house EVLB in Bruges, Belgium, designed by architect Vincent Van Duysen; **13l** Mark Smith's home in the Cotswolds; **13ar** Michael D'Souza of Mufti; **13br** The owner of Tessuti, Catherine Vindevogel-Debal's house in Kortrijk, Belgium; **14** Claire Haithwaite and Dean Maryon's home in Amsterdam; **15** Alfredo Paredes and Brad Goldfarb's loft in Tribeca, New York designed by Michael Neumann Architecture; **16** Michael D'Souza of Mufti; **17** Wendy Jansen and Chris Van Eldik, owners of J.O.B. Interieur's house in Wijk bij Duurstede, The Netherlands; **18** The Fitzwilliam-Lay's family home. Architecture by Totem Design, interior design by Henri Fitzwilliam-Lay and Totem Design; **19** Interior designer Timothy Whealon's Manhattan apartment; **20–21** The Meiré family home, designed by Marc Meiré; **22** The Campbell family's apartment in London, architecture by Voon Wong Architects; **22–23** The owner of Tessuti, Catherine Vindevogel-Debal's house in Kortrijk, Belgium. Kitchen designed by Filip Van Bever; **23r** Designer Tricia Foley's Long Island home; **24–25** The New York home of Gael Towey, Creative Director of Martha Stewart Living Omnimedia and Stephen Doyle, Creative Director of Doyle Partners; **26a** A family home in Parsons Green, London. Architecture by Nicholas Helm and Yasuyuki Fukuda (architectural assistant) of Helm Architects. Interior design and all material finishes supplied by Maria Speake of Retrouvius Reclamation & Design; **26b** & **27** Wendy Jansen and Chris Van Eldik, owners of J.O.B. Interieur's house in Wijk bij Duurstede, The Netherlands; **28** Interior designer Timothy Whealon's Manhattan apartment; **30a** Designer Tricia Foley's Long Island home; **30b** Alfredo Paredes and Brad Goldfarb's loft in Tribeca, New York designed by Michael Neumann Architecture; **31** The Meiré family home, designed by Marc Meiré; **32–37** The family house EVLB in Bruges, Belgium, designed by architect Vincent Van Duysen; **38** The owner of Tessuti, Catherine Vindevogel-Debal's house in Kortrijk, Belgium. Kitchen designed by Filip Van Bever; **39a** Claire Haithwaite and Dean Maryon's home in Amsterdam; **39b** The family house EVLB in Bruges, Belgium, designed by architect Vincent Van Duysen; **40** Mark Smith's home in the Cotswolds; **41** Sophie Eadie's family home in London; **42a** The New York home of Gael Towey, Creative Director of Martha Stewart Living Omnimedia and Stephen Doyle, Creative Director of Doyle Partners; **42b** The Campbell family's apartment in London, architecture by Voon Wong Architects; **43–44** A family home in Parsons Green, London. Architecture by Nicholas Helm and Yasuyuki Fukuda (architectural assistant) of Helm Architects. Interior design and all material finishes supplied by Maria Speake of Retrouvius Reclamation & Design; **45al** The Campbell family's apartment in London, architecture by Voon Wong Architects; **45ac** Alfredo Paredes and Brad Goldfarb's loft in Tribeca, New York designed by Michael Neumann Architecture; **45ar** Interior decorator and designer for the firm Sibyl Colefax & John Fowler, Philip Hooper's own flat in London; **45b** Wendy Jansen and Chris Van Eldik, owners of J.O.B. Interieur's house in Wijk bij Duurstede, The Netherlands; **46al** The Fitzwilliam-Lay's family home. Architecture by Totem Design, interior design by Henri Fitzwilliam-Lay and Totem Design; **46ac** Mark Smith's home in the Cotswolds; **46ar** Alfredo Paredes and Brad Goldfarb's loft in Tribeca, New York designed by Michael Neumann Architecture; **46b** The Campbell family's apartment in London, architecture by Voon Wong Architects; **47l** Interior decorator and designer for the firm Sibyl Colefax & John Fowler, Philip Hooper's own flat in London; **47ar** & **br** The Campbell family's apartment in London, architecture by Voon Wong Architects; **47bl** Mark Smith's home in the Cotswolds; **48l** & **49bl** Alfredo Paredes and Brad Goldfarb's loft in Tribeca, New York designed by Michael Neumann Architecture; **48–49** The family house EVLB in Bruges, Belgium, designed by architect Vincent Van Duysen; **48b** Sophie Eadie's family home in London; **49br** The Campbell family's apartment in London, architecture by Voon Wong Architects; **50l** Alfredo Paredes and Brad Goldfarb's loft in Tribeca, New York designed by Michael Neumann Architecture; **50r** The New York home of Gael Towey, Creative Director of Martha Stewart Living Omnimedia and Stephen Doyle, Creative Director of Doyle Partners; **51** Interior designer Timothy Whealon's Manhattan apartment. Lithographs 'Untitled', 1998 by artist Agnes Martin; **52** Mark Smith's home in the Cotswolds; **53al** Sophie Eadie's family home in London; **53ar** Michael D'Souza of Mufti; **53b** Angela and David Coxon's family home in Kent; **54a** Interior designer Timothy Whealon's Manhattan apartment; **54b** The Campbell family's apartment in London, architecture by Voon Wong Architects; **55al** & **c** Mark Smith's home in the Cotswolds; **55ar** The Fitzwilliam-Lay's family home. Architecture by Totem Design, interior design by Henri Fitzwilliam-Lay and Totem Design; **55bl** & **bcl** The Campbell family's apartment in London, architecture by Voon Wong Architects; **55bcr** The family house EVLB in Bruges, Belgium, designed by architect Vincent Van Duysen; **55br** The owner of Tessuti, Catherine Vindevogel-Debal's house in Kortrijk, Belgium; **56** Angela and David Coxon's family home in Kent; **57** The

Fitzwilliam-Lay's family home. Architecture by Totem Design, interior design by Henri Fitzwilliam-Lay and Totem Design; **58l** The New York home of Gael Towey, Creative Director of Martha Stewart Living Omnimedia and Stephen Doyle, Creative Director of Doyle Partners; **58–59** Sophie Eadie's family home in London; **59al** The Campbell family's apartment in London, architecture by Voon Wong Architects; **59r** Alfredo Paredes and Brad Goldfarb's loft in Tribeca, New York designed by Michael Neumann Architecture; **60b** Wendy Jansen and Chris Van Eldik, owners of J.O.B. Interieur's house in Wijk bij Duurstede, The Netherlands; **60a** & **61** Claire Haithwaite and Dean Maryon's home in Amsterdam; **62l** The owner of Tessuti, Catherine Vindevogel-Debal's house in Kortrijk, Belgium; **62ar** & **62–63** Sophie Eadie's family home in London; **62b** The family house EVLB in Bruges, Belgium, designed by architect Vincent Van Duysen; **63r** The Campbell family's apartment in London, architecture by Voon Wong Architects; **64** Wendy Jansen and Chris Van Eldik, owners of J.O.B. Interieur's house in Wijk bij Duurstede, The Netherlands; **65** Interior designer Timothy Whealon's Manhattan apartment; **66** Wendy Jansen and Chris Van Eldik, owners of J.O.B. Interieur's house in Wijk bij Duurstede, The Netherlands; **67ar** Interior decorator and designer for the firm Sibyl Colefax & John Fowler, Philip Hooper's own flat in London; **67b** Angela and David Coxon's family home in Kent; **68** Mark Smith's home in the Cotswolds; **69** Sophie Eadie's family home in London; **70–71** Michael D'Souza of Mufti; **72al** Wendy Jansen and Chris Van Eldik, owners of J.O.B. Interieur's house in Wijk bij Duurstede, The Netherlands; **72ar** & **b** Alfredo Paredes and Brad Goldfarb's loft in Tribeca, New York designed by Michael Neumann Architecture; **73** Interior designer Timothy Whealon's Manhattan apartment; **74–75** A family home in Parsons Green, London. Architecture by Nicholas Helm and Yasuyuki Fukuda (architectural assistant) of Helm Architects. Interior design and all material finishes supplied by Maria Speake of Retrouvius Reclamation & Design; **76–77** The owner of Tessuti, Catherine Vindevogel-Debal's house in Kortrijk, Belgium; **77r** Interior decorator and designer for the firm Sibyl Colefax & John Fowler, Philip Hooper's own flat in London; **78** Claire Haithwaite and Dean Maryon's home in Amsterdam; **79** Wendy Jansen and Chris Van Eldik, owners of J.O.B. Interieur's house in Wijk bij Duurstede, The Netherlands; **80–81** Interior decorator and designer for the firm Sibyl Colefax & John Fowler, Philip Hooper's own flat in London; **82–87** The Fitzwilliam-Lay's family home. Architecture by Totem Design, interior design by Henri Fitzwilliam-Lay and Totem Design; **88** Alfredo Paredes and Brad Goldfarb's loft in Tribeca, New York designed by Michael Neumann Architecture; **89l** The Fitzwilliam-Lay's family home. Architecture by Totem Design, interior design by Henri Fitzwilliam-Lay and Totem Design; **89r** Interior decorator and designer for the firm Sibyl Colefax & John Fowler, Philip Hooper's own flat in London; **90–91** A family home in Parsons Green, London. Architecture by Nicholas Helm and Yasuyuki Fukuda (architectural assistant) of Helm Architects. Interior design and all material finishes supplied by Maria Speake of Retrouvius Reclamation & Design; **92** Mark Smith's home in the Cotswolds; **93** Interior designer Timothy Whealon's Manhattan apartment; **94** Alfredo Paredes and Brad Goldfarb's loft in Tribeca, New York designed by Michael Neumann Architecture; **95** The Campbell family's apartment in London, architecture by Voon Wong Architects; **96** Interior designer Timothy Whealon's Manhattan apartment; **97** A family home in Parsons Green, London. Architecture by Nicholas Helm and Yasuyuki Fukuda (architectural assistant) of Helm Architects. Interior design and all material finishes supplied by Maria Speake of Retrouvius Reclamation & Design; **98** The owner of Tessuti, Catherine Vindevogel-Debal's house in Kortrijk, Belgium; **99** A family home in Parsons Green, London. Architecture by Nicholas Helm and Yasuyuki Fukuda (architectural assistant) of Helm Architects. Interior design and all material finishes supplied by Maria Speake of Retrouvius Reclamation & Design; **100l** The Meiré family home, designed by Marc Meiré; **100r** The New York home of Gael Towey, Creative Director of Martha Stewart Living Omnimedia and Stephen Doyle, Creative Director of Doyle Partners; **101** A family home in Parsons Green, London. Architecture by Nicholas Helm and Yasuyuki Fukuda (architectural assistant) of Helm Architects. Interior design and all material finishes supplied by Maria Speake of Retrouvius Reclamation & Design; **102** The Meiré family home, designed by Marc Meiré; **103b** The New York home of Gael Towey, Creative Director of Martha Stewart Living Omnimedia and Stephen Doyle, Creative Director of Doyle Partners; **103a** Interior designer Timothy Whealon's Manhattan apartment; **104al** Designer Tricia Foley's Long Island home; **104ar** Interior designer Timothy Whealon's Manhattan apartment; **104b** The Meiré family home, designed by Marc Meiré; **105** & **106l** Mark Smith's home in the Cotswolds; **106ar** Michael D'Souza of Mufti; **106br** Sophie Eadie's family home in London; **107** Claire Haithwaite and Dean Maryon's home in Amsterdam; **108–109** Interior designer Timothy Whealon's Manhattan apartment; **109r** Alfredo Paredes and Brad Goldfarb's loft in Tribeca, New York designed by Michael Neumann Architecture; **110–111** Interior decorator and designer for the firm Sibyl Colefax & John Fowler, Philip Hooper's own flat in London; **112** The New York home of Gael Towey, Creative Director of Martha Stewart Living Omnimedia and Stephen Doyle, Creative Director of Doyle Partners; **113** Sophie Eadie's family home in London; **114–115** Michael D'Souza of Mufti; **116** Claire Haithwaite and Dean Maryon's home in Amsterdam; **117a** A family home in Parsons Green, London. Architecture by Nicholas Helm and Yasuyuki Fukuda (architectural assistant) of Helm Architects. Interior design and all material finishes supplied by Maria Speake of Retrouvius Reclamation & Design; **117b** Interior decorator and designer for the firm Sibyl Colefax & John Fowler, Philip Hooper's own flat in London; **118a** & **119al** Alfredo Paredes and Brad Goldfarb's loft in Tribeca, New York designed by Michael Neumann Architecture; **118b** The New York home of Gael Towey, Creative Director of Martha Stewart Living Omnimedia and Stephen Doyle, Creative Director of Doyle Partners; **119bl** & **r** The Campbell family's apartment in London, architecture by Voon Wong Architects; **120** & **121l** Wendy Jansen and Chris Van Eldik, owners of J.O.B. Interieur's house in Wijk bij Duurstede, The Netherlands; **121r** Sophie Eadie's family home in London; **122a** Mark Smith's home in the Cotswolds; **122b** The Campbell family's apartment in London, architecture by Voon Wong Architects; **123** Michael D'Souza of Mufti; **124–125** The New York home of Gael Towey, Creative Director of Martha Stewart Living Omnimedia and Stephen Doyle, Creative Director of Doyle Partners; **126** The owner of Tessuti, Catherine Vindevogel-Debal's house in Kortrijk, Belgium. Kitchen designed by Filip Van Bever; **127** Angela and David Coxon's family home in Kent; **128–129a** A family home in Parsons Green, London. Architecture by Nicholas Helm and Yasuyuki Fukuda (architectural assistant) of Helm Architects. Interior design and all material finishes supplied by Maria Speake of Retrouvius Reclamation & Design; **129b** The Fitzwilliam-Lay's family home. Architecture by Totem Design, interior design by Henri Fitzwilliam-Lay and Totem Design; **130–131** The Meiré family home, designed by Marc Meiré; **132–137** Designer Tricia Foley's Long Island home.

architects and designers featured in this book

Stephen Doyle
Creative Director of Doyle Partners
1123 Broadway at 25th Street
New York NY 10010
USA
+1 212 463 8787

www.doylepartners.com

*Pages 24–25, 42a, 50r, 58l, 100r,
103b, 112, 118b, 124–125*

Henri Fitzwilliam-Lay
Interior Design

Hfitz@hotmail.com

Also involved in this project:

Carpentry/Joinery:

Nick Hudson
Worton Hall Trading Estate
Worton Road
Isleworth
Middlesex TW7 6ER
020 8847 3535

*Pages 4, 18, 46al, 55ar, 57, 82–87,
89l, 129b*

Tricia Foley
Designer
+1 212 348 0074
fax +1 212 423 9146

triciafoley@erols.com

*Pages 11b, 23r 30a, 104al,
132–137*

Helm Architects
2 Montagu Row
London W1U 6DX
020 7224 1884
fax 020 7224 1885

nh@helmarchitects.com

*Pages 2–3, 6, 26a, 44, 74–75,
90–91, 97, 99, 101, 117a, 128,
129a*

J.O.B. Interieur
Dijkstraat 5
3961 AA Wijk bij Duurstede
The Netherlands
+31 343 578818
fax +31 343 578157

JOBINT@xs4all.nl

*Pages 9r, 17, 26b, 27, 45b, 60b,
64, 66, 72al, 79, 120, 121l*

Marc Meiré

Meirefamily@aol.com

*Pages 20–21, 31, 100l, 102, 104b,
130–131*

Michael Neumann Architecture
11 East 88th Street
New York NY 10128
USA
+1 212 828 0407

www.mnarch.com

Principal: Michael Neumann
Project Manager: Jairo Camelo
Design Team: Talin Rudy

Also involved in this project:

Design Consultant: John Heist
Woodwork: Daniel DeMarco
Kitchen: Metal Master
Metal walls: Face Design

*Pages 15, 30b, 45ac, 46ar, 48l,
49bl, 50l, 59r, 72ar & b, 88, 94,
109r, 118a, 119al*

Mufti
789 Fulham Road
London SW6 5HA
020 7610 9123
fax 020 7384 2050

www.mufti.co.uk

*Pages 10–11, 11a, 13ar, 16, 53ar
70–71, 106ar, 114–115, 123*

Retrouvius Reclamation & Design
2A Ravensworth Road
Kensal Green
London NW10 5NR
tel/fax 020 8960 6060

mail@retrouvius.com
www.retrouvius.com

Also involved in this project:

Agnes Emery
Emery & Cie
Noir D'Ivoire
Rue de l'Hôpital 25–29
1000 Bruxelles
Belgium
+32 2 513 58 92
fax +32 2 513 39 70

*Moroccan tiles, concrete floor tiles,
selected paints.*

Paul Simmons
Timorous Beasties
7 Craigend Place
Anniesland
Glasgow G13 2UN
0141 9593331

Bespoke, hand-printed textiles.

*Pages 2–3, 6, 26a, 44, 74–75,
90–91, 97, 99, 101, 117a, 128,
129a*

Sibyl Colefax & John Fowler
39 Brook Street
London W1K 4JE
020 7493 2231
fax 020 7355 4037

*Pages 5, 45ar, 47l, 67ar, 77r,
80–81, 89r, 110–111, 117b*

Mark Smith at Smithcreative
15 St George's Road
London W4 1AU
020 8747 3909
fax 020 8742 3902

mark@smithcreative.net

Ceramics by David Garland 01285 720307

*Pages 13l, 40, 46ac, 47bl, 52, 55al
& c, 68, 92, 106l, 122a*

Angela Southwell
Interior Design
01732 763246

angsouthwell@hotmail.com

Also featured in this home:

Maybury
126 Oxford Street
Woodstock
Oxon OX20 1TZ
01993 813334

www.mayburydesign.co.uk

*Tropical rustic furniture and
accessories.*

Pages 53b, 56, 67b, 127

Tessuti
Interiors & Fabrics
Doorniksewijk 76
8500 Kortrijk
Belgium
+32 56 25 29 27

info@tessuti.be
www.tessuti.be

*Pages endpapers, 12a, 13br, 22–23,
38, 55br, 62l, 76–77, 98, 126*

Timothy Whealon Inc.
23 East 69th Street, #2
New York NY 10021
USA
+1 212 249 2153
fax +1 212 249 2472

tjwhealon@tjwdesigns.com

*Pages 19, 28, 51, 54a, 65, 73, 93,
96, 103a, 104ar, 108–109*

Totem Design
Ian Hume
2 Alexander Street
London W2 5NT
020 7243 0692

totem.uk@virgin.net

*Pages 4, 18, 46al, 55ar, 57, 82–87,
89l, 129b*

Filip Van Bever
Kitchen Design

Filipvanbever@skynet.be

Pages 22–23, 38, 126

Vincent Van Duysen Architects
Lombardenvest 34
2000 Antwerp
Belgium
+32 3 205 91 90
fax +32 3 204 01 38

vincent@vincentvanduysen.com
www.vincentvanduysen.com

*Pages 1, 12b, 32–37, 39b, 48–49,
44bcr, 62b*

Voon Wong Architects
Unit 27
1 Stannary Street
London SE11 4AD
020 7587 0116
fax 020 7840 0178

voon@btconnect.com

*Pages 8, 22, 42b, 45al, 46b, 47ar &
br, 49br, 54b, 55bl & bcl, 59al, 63r,
95, 119bl & r, 122b*

index

acknowledgments

Thank you to Alison Starling and David Peters at Ryland Peters & Small, for
backing a book about vital first thoughts and plans, not just finishing touches.
To my agent, Fiona Lindsay of Limelight Management, for her candid advice
and enthusiasm, and especially to Clare Double, for being a patient and
talented editor.

Thanks, Jan, for taking gorgeous photos, and being fun to be with. To Gabriella
Le Grazie and Paul Tilby, for subtle art direction, and to Claire Hector, for
winkling out great locations. And to every homeowner we visited, thanks
for letting us share your personal vision of tranquillity!

Thank you darling Cicely and Felix, for staying cheery whilst I was away
shooting and writing the book, and to my parents, Harry and Ann, for
continued support. And a special thanks to Anthony, who taught me that
perfect planning is *always* worth the effort, because it guarantees
a harmonious home.